CALLED FOR BLESSINGS

Experiencing Calvary's Blessings

CALLED FOR BLESSINGS

Experiencing Calvary's Blessings

James Ekor-Tah

Publishing today for tomorrow's generation

© 2012 by James Ekor-Tah

Published by Perez Publishing LLC – *www.perezpublishing.com* –

For your questions and publishing needs write to:

Perez Publishing
548 Congressional Drive
Westminster, MD, 21158
USA
Email: *perezpublishing@gmail.com*

Printed in the United States of America

All rights reserved. No part of this publication may be reproduced, stored in a retrieval system, or transmitted in any form or by any means — for example, electronic, photocopy, recording — without the prior written permission of the publisher. The only exception is brief quotations in printed reviews.

James Ekor-Tah

To contact the author, write to:

James Ekor-Tah
Email: *ekortah@gmail.com*

Called for Blessings / James Ekor-Tah

ISBN: 978-0-9850668-2-6

Unless otherwise indicated, all Scripture quotations are taken from the New King James Version of the Bible. Copyright © 1979, 1980, 1982, by Thomas Nelson, Inc. Used by permission. All rights reserved.

Scripture quotations marked NIV are taken from the Holy Bible: New International Version ˚ NIV ˚. Copyright © 1973, 1978, 1984 by International Bible Society. Used by permission of Zondervan Publishing House. All rights reserved.

The author has emphasized some words in Scripture quotation in underlined type.

Cover Image: Carden's Design Photography Services, used by permission.

Cover/Interior Design: Zach Essama - *graphicspartner@gmail.com*

Contents

Dedication vii
Acknowledgement ix
Foreword xi
Introduction xiii

Chapter 1: What Is Life? 15
Chapter 2: Salvation Journey 21
Chapter 3: The Source of Life 31
Chapter 4: Who Are You? 39
Chapter 5: The Atoning Work of Christ 49
Chapter 6: Knowing God 61
Chapter 7: The Goodness of God 69
Chapter 8: God our Father 77
Chapter 9: The Grace of God 87
Chapter 10: Called for Blessings 97

About the Author 109

Dedication

To my precious family:

Elizabeth Grace and Madeleine Shekinah, and my dear wife Julienne Abigail.

Acknowledgement

All the glory goes to my precious Savior, The Lord Jesus, who is forever blessed. I thank You Lord for your grace which enabled me to complete this work.

I thank my wife Julienne Abigail who is a living witness to the power of the messages in this book. Sweetheart, thank you for being the first person God used to show me the transforming power of these messages. Called for Blessings is a result of your constant reminder and encouragements to share these truths with the larger body of believers.

I want to say a special thank you to the members of my local congregation of CMFI-Riverdale MD. The changes I saw in your lives were a big motivating factor behind the publication of this book. It's a privilege to serve as your pastor.

My gratitude to my dear friend, Rev. Robinson Fondong, Senior Pastor of CMFI Westminster, for your friendship and support in the ministry. I appreciate you and your ministry which God used to bring me to faith in Christ.

I will always remain grateful to Rev. Dr. Simon and Grace Epamba who adopted me as their son. The seed you sowed into my life has grown into this prevailing work of God.

Thank you Pastor Darrel Baer of Franklin Mennonite Conference, for the father role you play in championing me in the ministry. I appreciate your unfeigned encouragements and support. In the same trend, I say thank you Kathy Hicks for being the mother that you are. Your motherly investments have paid off. May God richly reward you.

Finally, a word of gratitude to the following individuals for your love and support towards the realization of this work: Paule Esther and Jesse Peaker, Moses and Dr. Esther Gwan, Roger and Vicky Nkembe, Celestine Nakeli, Paul and Adriel Kempa, Elizabeth and Marc Desire.

Foreword

The spiritual life is a relationship journey where we encounter the presence of God and the meaning of our salvation in ever growing dimensions. It is significant in this book that James describes the blessings of salvation from his own spiritual journey as well as the academic/logical teachings from scripture.

Modern evangelical Christianity has dominated the public language with a description of salvation as being saved *"from"* something – namely sin and hell. While that is biblically true and should never be diminished, it leaves a gap in the salvation theology about how it affects the meaning of living. To come to experience salvation as gaining access into a new and empowering relationship with our loving, creator God is a powerful revelation that sets our spirits free to live life to its fullest. It's the difference between living life in the binding shadow of the power of sin and its consequences, or living life in the bright light of the throne of God. In this book the author attempts to show us how the scripture describes salvation as restoring us into the fullness of life with God, even while not yet fully restored.

While this blessing of God is offered and provided for us, we need to reach out and receive it. This book calls us to hear scripture in such a way that our faith is challenged to live into all that God desires for us. This requires a clearly focused love of God and a faith that is willing to name God's blessings and live into their fullness. In this way our life has significant meaning and our calling has great reward.

Thank you, James, for sharing your personal revelations and spiritual joy with us all.

>Darrell Baer
>Conference Minister,
>Franklin Mennonite Conference

Introduction

God first began to show me the blessings of Calvary in 1995. One morning, during my regular devotion, while I was singing a chorus by the popular Voice of the Cross Singers: *"all the way to Calvary He went for me, He died to set me free."* I could visualize the agony of Jesus from the Garden of Gethsemane all through to the crucifixion. Then, I saw myself standing at the foot of the cross looking at Jesus on that cross. I could see myself crucified with Christ while looking at Him. This happened in flashes of short mental images. And it was such a moving experience to the extent that I felt as though I was amongst the crowd on that crucifixion day. Tears run down my cheeks as I sobbed uncontrollably.

This encounter with God happened many years before the movie; *"The Passion of Christ"* was produced. But my experience was as graphic as some of the scenes in that movie.

Immediately after this wonderful experience, an inexplicable love and peace from God enveloped my emotions and I felt as though I was floating. I knew for sure that Jesus loves me and that He cares about me enough to die for my freedom; freedom from the eternal consequences of my sins, the power of sin and from the powers of darkness. This then was the beginning of my quest into understanding what the mission of Jesus to earth was all about.

In the book you are about to read, I have shared some truths that will help you on the path to experiencing the blessings of Calvary. These truths have impacted my life and I trust that the same will happen to you. My appeal to you is that you approach the Word of God with simplicity of heart; for therein is the power of God revealed. Jesus once said, *"Are you not in error because you do not know the Scriptures or the power of God?"* (Mark 12:24)

In 2 Corinthians 5:17 the Bible says, *"Therefore, if anyone is in Christ, he is a new creation; old things have passed away; behold, all things have become new."* And also remember that, *"God is faithful, by whom you were called into the fellowship of His Son, Jesus Christ our Lord."* (1 Corinthians 1:9)

I strongly believe that a progressive revelation of God in you, through His Son Jesus, will be granted to you; even as I have attempted to communicate in this book. May God's richest blessings in Christ be your experience. Amen.

Chapter 1

WHAT IS LIFE?

Jesus said: "I have come that they may have life, and that they may have it more abundantly."
(John 10:10)

I had promised writing a poem for Julienne.[1] So, as I took some time to be still and quiet down my heart and mind, the question: *"What is life?"* began to ring in my heart. I quickly jotted down the thoughts that were flowing; after which I gave myself some time of meditation on the lines I had written. And as a result, the following poem was written.

---

1 Julienne and I are married, but this was before we got married.

What is life?

Life is responsibility.

Life offers us rights and rights come with duty.

And it's in the execution of our duties that we exercise our rights. Rights are the benefits of responsibility. And responsibility creates opportunities for discovery in life.

Life is opportunities.

Life comes with the potential for advancement.

If we prepare ourselves, we will make the most of opportunities in life. And opportunities make a way for achievement when they do come our way.

Life is a choice.

What we make out of life is tied to our choices.

Our choices today determine our tomorrow.

Let our choices for today have our tomorrow in view. Our life is the sum total of our choices.

Life is a personal race.

You know, in a race, there always is discipline.

So, in life, our success is largely influenced by our discipline. Our Life has no match with another's but lessons learnt are valuable gems. Therefore be focused.

Life is a gift.

Life is an endowment but never fair. Get to know who we are and our talents, then life will make sense.

A gift is never earned, it is received so as to possess.
Only then, is its full benefits appreciated and enjoyed.

Life is relationships.
Life is a direct result of the quality of relationships we have. So, invest in relationships and be wise in doing so. We're where we are due to relationships with people. Let's Take care of our relationships. Be a people person.

Life is a challenge.
There always will be room for improvement.
Make the necessary adjustments that lead the way forward. Measure your goals and meet up with the challenges. And never shy away from a challenge.

To Julienne, my love!
Nov 06, 2005
Worcester, South Africa.

What is my Life all about?

Tom Blandi – 1907 French Literary Theorist author, once said: *"Our attitudes control our lives. Attitudes are a secret power working twenty-four hours a day, for good or bad. It is of paramount importance that we know how to harness and control this great force."* Someone has defined attitude as: *"A composite of our thoughts which cause our feelings which express our actions. Thoughts, feelings and actions when in sync, define our attitude".*

In the Bible, Moses admonished the Israelites in regards to their attitude about life saying, *"Now what I am commanding you today is not too difficult for you or beyond your reach. It is not up in heaven, so that you have to ask, 'Who will ascend to heaven to get it and proclaim it to us so that we may obey it?' Nor is it beyond the sea so that you have to ask, 'Who will cross the sea to get it and proclaim it to us so that we may obey it?' No, the word is near you; it is in your mouth and in your heart so that you may obey it."*

> See, I set before you today life and prosperity, death and destruction. For I command you today to love the LORD your God, to walk in his ways, and to keep his commands, decrees and laws; then you will live and increase, and the LORD your God will bless you in the land you are entering to possess.
>
> But if your heart turns away and you are not obedient, and if you are drawn away to bow down to other gods and worship them, I declare to you this day that you will certainly be destroyed. You will not live long in the land you are crossing the Jordan to enter and possess.
>
> This day I call heaven and earth as witness against you that I have set before you life and death, blessings and curses. Now choose life, so that you and your children may live and that you may love the LORD your God, listen to his voice, and hold fast to him. For the LORD is your life, and he will give you many years in the land he swore to give to your fathers, Abraham, Isaac, and Jacob.
>
> (Deuteronomy 30:11-20 NIV)

Pay Attention

Everyone wishes to enjoy life and prosperity, and to flee death and evil. Everyone desires happiness, and dreads misery. But not many people understand that God's desire for them is that they may have and enjoy these things in their life. Very few have arrived to the conclusion that God is not against them but that He is for them.

You see, because we are trapped in the deception of sin and self-will – fruit of "the tree of the knowledge of good and evil", we think, feel and act in ways that say, *"I can do without God."* Yet, great is the compassion of the Lord that He comes to us through His Word; (God's blueprint for eternal redemption from *"the knowledge of good and evil"*), offering us access to the Tree of Life. God's Word is spirit and life and it is able[2] to bring us into the experience of abundant life; if it be not of our own fault by neglecting to pay attention.

If anyone would love God, and pay attention to His Word – *the Word of Life*[3], to do what He says, he would live and be blessed. If anyone should turn from God, depart from His Word, and worship other gods, that would certainly be to his ruin.

I encourage you to pay attention to God's Word. Choose life and enter into the blessings that are yours in Christ. In John 10:10 Jesus said: *"The thief does not come except to steal, and to kill, and to destroy. <u>I have come that they may have life</u>, and that they may have it more abundantly."* Jesus has not changed. He is the same yesterday, today and forever. He came just for you and He is willing to personally get involved with your plight so that you may have life more abundantly. But He would not do

---

2 James 1:21
3 1 John 1:1

anything without your cooperation. Do you believe in Him? Act now and ask Him to help you.

My Prayer to the Lord

Dear Lord Jesus,

I want to know Your will for my life. I am not very sure about it, but I know that it is good. Again it's been my reluctance to seek You with all my heart. I have tried my own ways all these years. My heart had not been focused on Your will but it has been full of my own thoughts, plans and ways. I am sorry for all the wasted years of my life. Please forgive me. I repent now.

Lord, I give You my will; help me to know Your calling for my life. Use this book to reveal yourself to me in a new way. I open my heart before You so that Your love may fill it and set it ablaze with passion for You. O Lord, that I may know you and the power of your resurrection.

Thank You for Your love and patience towards me. Amen.

Chapter 2

SALVATION JOURNEY

1987 was the year I went to secondary school (i.e. middle school). It was an exciting time for me, but I happened to be the only pupil from my former school that was in my class of *"Form 1 C"* (6th or 7th Grade). Everything was new to me and my new desk mate, Robinson Fondong, was the *"Assistant Class Prefect."* I, being a *"noise maker"*, my friendship with him was beneficial to me in the sense that I would not be listed for punishment every time I was noisy in class. So, Robinson would warn me every now and then to stop being noisy.

My new friend was also a good story teller. Though I did not like his stories because they were religious and unexciting to me, he was the only person I had to hang out with. Our break time was spent together during which he will often tell stories about the Bible and the like. He would ask me to pray with him before we ate. He would pray out loud and I will just mumble a few phrases of the Lord's Prayer under my breath. But my friend would just talk to God directly as if God was right there with us. He would pray and always end his prayer by saying *"in Jesus name, Amen."*

One year had gone by and this friendship with Robinson grew stronger. And as a result, I changed my route from school to home. I had to walk home with him after school during which he would tell us some stories he had read. I remember how on one afternoon he told us the story of Kenneth E. Hagin's near death experience and how he was miraculously healed. This story really touched me. No one had ever described hell to me in such a dramatic way before.

I was convicted of sin and my lost condition without Christ in my life. Many days later Robinson asked me if I wanted Christ in my heart. I said yes. He then prayed with me and I received Jesus as my Savior for the very first time.

I wanted to go to heaven when Jesus returns. That was my need at that time and I was glad to have received His forgiveness and my life was radically transformed. The inexplicable joy and peace of God flooded my soul. I knew that my sins were forgiven and my name was written in the Lamb's Book of Life.

Salvation for me meant that I will be accepted in heaven when I die or if Jesus returns before death I will be *"raptured"* with all the saints. That was the popular understanding of salvation at the time and I lived out my faith basically focusing on obeying the Lord, living sacrificially for Him, doing His commandments as a good disciple so that I may have treasures and rewards in heaven. *"Well done good and faithful servant"*[4] was a very familiar Scripture.

Very little thought was given to life on earth apart from the one ambition to evangelize the whole world and get everybody saved so that we can all be out of here at Jesus' return. This world to me was very sinful and corrupt and I could not possibly be investing any part of my life in it. But, it was not too long after my initial salvation experience that I found myself in the midst of a fierce struggle within my soul.

My Struggle

In John 3:16 Jesus said, *"For God so loved the world that He gave His only begotten Son, that whoever believes in Him should not perish but have everlasting life."*

For some reason I could not understand this verse beyond the fact that Jesus was sent so that if I believed in Him, I would not perish in hell but have eternal life and go to heaven. I think that I got a grasp of the perishing part of this verse and I did not want anything to do with hell. On the other hand I got a partial understanding with the eternal life part, because I thought that it was a benefit for the future.

I thought that the reason I was saved at a young age was so that I could serve God with my whole life and lay up treasures in heaven for a better and rewarding life after death.

---

[4] Matthew 25:23

"Thank God I shall no more die the second death[5] for I have passed from death unto life[6]." Of course, that was settled (*i.e. I shall no more die the second death*) and my salvation was complete in view of the fact that I had been baptized by immersion and had received the baptism with the Holy Spirit.

My struggles though, were in my lack of knowledge and understanding concerning the *"salvation of the now,"* which is, *"I have passed from death unto life"* as a present tense reality. I was very sure that my past sins were washed away but was not very sure that I was accepted and pleasing to God at all times in the now and here; given that I had to always confess all sins and put them under the blood so that I would be ready for Jesus' return.

The burden of salvation for the now and here was my responsibility. I thought that I had to *"work out my salvation with fear and trembling[7]"* and attain through my efforts.

Sermons I heard on, *"salvation as a free gift"* were limited to the initial born again experience. Therefore my experience was that it was very costly trying to please God as a Christian and failing to measure-up all the time. You must *"pay the price"* was a common phrase in the language of the church folks of the day.

Please, don't get me wrong, I believe in *"paying the price"* as part of the Christian walk. Some things in life only come our way in exchange for others. Self denial is not cheap. The

---

5   Revelation 20:6
6   1 John 3:14
7   Philippians 1:12

anointing for ministry is costly and there is a cost for true discipleship. But I could not determine which part of salvation was free and which required a price to be paid by me in order to satisfy the heart of God. Thus the confusion I was in.

This struggle with trying to please God and failing to do so then became a circle. And it went on like that for many years. Romans chapter 7:19 which says, *"For the good that I will to do, I do not do; but the evil I will not to do, that I practice."* describes exactly what my experience was.

I searched for answers from the leaders of the church by asking questions and reading many books from the church library and other books that were recommended by those who have been following the Lord for a longer time before me.

Praise God, the day came when I experienced another *"phase of salvation."*

The Enlightenment

> But now having been set free from sin, and having become slaves of God, you have your fruit to holiness, and the end, everlasting life. For the wages of sin is death, but the gift of God is eternal life in Christ Jesus our Lord.
> (Romans 6:22-23)

One day, as I was reading my Bible, the above passage was illuminated in my spirit-man. Even though I had received forgiveness of my sins, I was unconsciously trying to earn eternal life. Romans 6:23 says, *"the wages of sin is death but the gift of God is eternal life in Christ Jesus our Lord."*

As I read this verse, my eyes were opened and it was instantly clear to me that eternal life is a gift of God in Christ Jesus and not a wage. It can not be earned. I thought in my mind saying, *"You see, eternal life and death can not possibly cohabit. It is either one or the other."* And my mind clicked with a resounding yes from my spirit-man. So, I read verse 22 of Romans 6 which says, *"But now having been set free from sin, and having become slaves of God, you have your fruit to holiness, and the end, eternal life."*

Romans 6:22 teaches that I have been set free from sin. So, salvation is not just about the forgiveness of sin but also the deliverance from sin. My sins were washed away and I have been freed from the power of sin. The fruit of my life is now holiness. Therefore, it is now my nature to be holy. Hallelujah! Amen.

Through faith, this truth became a present tense experience for me. O yes, *"Now faith is the substance of things hoped for, the evidence of things not seen."* (Hebrews 11:1) And *"Faith comes by hearing and hearing by the word of God."* (Romans 10:17) Wow! This is good news!!

Eternal life was a gift of God and I have received this gift in Christ Jesus. I have it now. It's not a future gift, it's a *now reality*. And *"I have passed from death unto life"* and not just *"I shall pass from death unto life."* Amen.

My heart was filled with indescribable peace. It was in a similar fashion like when I first received the forgiveness of my sins. Peace with God was now a personal testimony. *"And this is the testimony: that God <u>has given</u> us eternal life, and this life is* in His Son. He who has the Son *has life*; he who does not have the Son of God does not have life." (1 John 5:11-12)

The Life of Christ through the Holy Spirit on the insight of me empowers me to yield fruit to holiness. Yeah, Holiness is a fruit and not a root of my faith in Christ. So, the out working of my salvation is a result of me yielding fruits from the life within.

Now then, linking this truth with John 3:16, *("For God so loved the world that He gave His only begotten Son, that whoever believes in Him should not perish but have everlasting life.")* we see that God's gift (which is Jesus), was purposed to save the perishing soul of anyone who believes and to let that soul have the gift of eternal life which would cause him to *pass from death unto life,* (setting him free from sin) and to let him yield *fruits unto holiness.*

A born again believer has received a divine impartation of the gift of eternal life into his spirit. So, being born again is the means by which man's redemption from the power of the perishing force (i.e. sin) is wrought. Therefore, at salvation, the power of the perishing force was broken and eternal life imparted into the spirit of the believer. Hallelujah! Thank you Lord!!

> But as many as received Him, to them He gave the power to become children of God, to those who believe in His name: who were born, not of blood, nor of the will of the flesh, nor of the will of man, but of God.
>
> (John 1:12-13)

Eternal life in Christ is then, the infusion of power from God which makes us become children of God. This is God's gift to all who put their faith in Christ Jesus. You and I were *"created according to God, in true righteousness and holiness"*[8] the very instant we received Christ and placed our faith in Him as our Savior.

Because Jesus died in our stead, we died; and as He was raised from the death so are we raised unto newness of life – eternal life (Zoë).

In Romans 5:1-2 the Bible says, *"Therefore, having been justified by faith, we have peace with God through our Lord Jesus Christ, through whom also we have access by faith into this grace in which we stand, and rejoice in hope of the glory of God."* God's glory could once more be a reality in and through my life. God's presence is now desired and enjoyed. And remember that access into this grace is by faith. For without faith it is impossible to please God.

The simple truths I just shared with you profoundly impacted my thinking and my understanding of salvation. My life was radically transformed. I was set free from the struggles of trying to please God by my own efforts. You know, salvation is God's plan to get lost souls back into a loving relationship with Himself through the blood of Jesus Christ.

The Hymn Writer, Daniel W. Whittle (1840-1901), wrote a hymn titled *"Redemption Ground."* This hymn best expressed my joy and gratitude to God for His wonderful plan of salvation.

---

[8] Ephesians 4:24

Salvation Journey

Come sing, my soul, and praise the Lord,
Who hath redeemed thee by His blood;
Delivered thee from chains that bound,
And brought thee to redemption ground.

Refrain:

Redemption ground, the ground of peace!
Redemption ground, O wondrous grace!
Here let our praise to God abound!
Who saves us on redemption ground.

Once from my God I wandered far,
And with His holy will made war;
But now my songs to God abound;
I'm standing on redemption ground.

O joyous hour! When God to me
A vision gave of Calvary;
My bonds were loosed – my soul unbound;
I sang upon redemption ground.

No words of merit now I plead,
But Jesus take for all my need;
No righteousness in me is found,
Except upon redemption ground.

Come, weary soul, and here find rest;
Accept redemption, and be blest;
The Christ who died, by God is crowned
To pardon on redemption ground.

At salvation, you and I received forgiveness of all our sins but we also received freedom from sin. The very moment we would yield our minds to the truth of God's word, is the same moment we experience the power of sin being broken in our life. Seeing truth internally will change your outward experience of life. For the law of the Spirit of life in Christ Jesus is operational.

> There is therefore now no condemnation to those who are in Christ Jesus, who do not walk according to the flesh, but according to the Spirit. For the law of the Spirit of life in Christ Jesus has made me free from the law of sin and death.
> (Romans 8:1-2)

Living out my salvation has become effortless, because it is now a fruit of the life of Christ in and through me. Paul the Apostle testifies to this fact saying, *"I have been crucified with Christ; it is no longer I who live, but Christ lives in me; and the life which I now live in the flesh I live by faith in the Son of God, who loved me and gave Himself for me. I do not set aside the grace of God; for if righteousness comes through the law, then Christ died in vain."* (Galatians 2:20-21)

Never forget that it was an exchange of life. He took your place so that you may have His life as a gift. Therefore enjoy. It's all yours now in Christ. Amen

Chapter 3

THE SOURCE OF LIFE

For by him were all things created, that are in heaven, and that are in earth, visible and invisible, whether they be thrones, or dominions, or principalities, or powers: all things were created by him, and for him.
(Colossians 1:16)

God is the Creator of all things. Everything that exists (visible or invisible, things that are known and those yet to be discovered by Mankind) was created by God and for Him. The first line of the Bible clearly says, *"In the beginning God created the heaven and the earth"* And in Psalm 102:25 it says, *"And, thou, Lord, in the beginning hast laid the foundation of the earth: and the heavens are the works of thine hands." (KJV)*

Therefore, we can see from Scriptures that, God who is the Creator of all things is also the undeniable Source of life. For, in Genesis 1:26-27, the Bible says,

> And God said, Let us make man in our image, after our likeness... So God created man in his own image, in the image of God created he him; male and female created he them.

So, we see that man was created in the image of God, inferring that Man was to be a reflection of God on earth. In the same way that our image in a mirror is a reflection of what we look like, Man was created to reflect God upon the earth. Hence, God created man in His own image and likeness so that he may function on the earth as an extension of Himself.

God is a Spirit. Therefore, Man must be a spirit being – like his Creator, though living in a physical body. God, the *Ultimate Creator,* created Man by drawing from His being, (i.e. from His image and likeness) and placed His divine qualities in Man. Thus creating Man with the potentials and abilities to operate and function on the earth as a *co-creator.*

God is the source of all of Man's creativity, imagination, knowledge, wisdom, abilities, skills etc. *"So God created man in his own image, in the image of God created he him; male and female created he them."* (Genesis 1:27)

The Sin Problem of Man

Someone may say, *"I get your point. 'God created man in his own image', but how would you explain the presence of evil in the world? Did God create evil?"*

The Source of Life

Well, God created Adam and Eve with all that they needed to be successful and to function on earth in the image and likeness of God. For God to be fair and be just to say that man was created in the image and likeness of God, He had to give Adam a *"free will."* God Himself possesses these qualities.[9] Thus Adam was created with the potential to make choices which at the same time meant that Adam was responsible in his capacity as ruler upon the earth. This was God's gift to Adam.

> And God said, Let us make man in our image, after our likeness: and let them have dominion over the fish of the sea, and over the fowl of the air, and over the cattle, and over all the earth, and over every creeping thing that creepeth upon the earth.
> (Genesis 1:26)

I would like to draw your attention to the fact that God created all things by speaking forth His Word. In Genesis 1, every day of the six days of creation started with; *"And God said."* This faculty of God was also placed in Adam and he actually functioned in this capacity when he named all the living creatures by speaking forth their names. The following account shows how it happened.

> And out of the ground the Lord God formed every beast of the field, and every fowl of the air and brought them to Adam to see what he would call them: and whatsoever Adam called every living creature, that was the name thereof.
> (Genesis 2:19 KJV)

---

9   Genesis 3:22 "Then the LORD God said, *"Behold, the man has become like one of Us, to know good and evil. And now, lest he put out his hand and take also of the tree of life, and eat, and live forever"*

Therefore, if all that exist was created by the Word of God and without the Word nothing was made that has been made, then God's Word must have a central place in the continuation of all that exist. For God is *"upholding all things by the word of his power." (Hebrews 1:3)*

In Romans 10:17 the Bible says, *"Faith cometh by hearing, and hearing by the word of God."* Therefore we may say that Adam and Eve were created to function by faith since they were created in the image of God who is the God of faith.

Man's relationship with God and as well as his dominion position over the rest of creation was to be maintained by Faith. Bible faith comes by hearing and hearing by the word of God. So God gave Adam His Word in a command, which is the basis for man's faith. This was God's design and it has not changed. We are related to God by faith. *"But without faith it is impossible to please him: for he that cometh to God must believe that he is, and that he is a rewarder of them that diligently seek him."* (Hebrews 11:6)

In Genesis 2:16-17, the Bible says, *"And the Lord God commanded the man, saying, Of every tree of the Garden thou mayest freely eat: but of the tree of the knowledge of good and evil thou shalt not eat for in the day that thou eatest thereof thou shalt surely die."*

Adam and Eve believed the Word of God and were thus rightly related to God and the rest of creation. They walked in the realm of faith and in the blessings of God. However, Adam and Eve were tempted by the devil and they chose to disbelieve God and ate of *"the tree of the knowledge of good and evil."* As a result of their disobedience to the command of God, sin and death entered into the world and with it, all the evil that we see today. See Genesis 3:1-19.

> Wherefore, as by one man sin entered into the world, and death by sin; and so death passed upon all men, for that all have sinned.
> (Romans 5:12)

The Necessity of God's Command

Again someone may ask: *"Was it necessary for God to give man this command?"*

We have seen that man was to live by faith and that Bible faith comes by hearing the word of God. Once more, do you remember our talk on how God created Man with the power of choice and free will and also that Man was to exercise his function and responsibility as ruler over the earth?

Well you would agree with me that where there is any type of responsibility invested upon anyone, there has to be some system of accountability. I believe that God gave Adam the command not to eat from *"the tree of the knowledge of good and evil"* as a warning to protect him from its corruptive power.

When tempted by the devil, the Lord Jesus answered and said, *"It is written, Man shall not live by bread alone, but by every word that proceedeth out of the mouth of God"* (Matthew 4:4 KJV)

The source of Man's life was from the Word that proceeded out of the mouth of God; and Man's existence was not to be sustained by bread alone but by every Word that proceeds out of the mouth of God. God's words are spirit and they are life. Jesus, who is the Word incarnate said, *"The thief does not come except to steal, and to kill, and to destroy. I have come that they may have life, and that they may have it more abundantly."* (John 10:10) Amen.

Can you see why the Word of God was very central in the life of Adam and why it is supposed to be central in your own life? Satan declared himself the enemy of Man by attacking the place of God's Word in his life. By so doing, he (Satan) has managed to steal, kill and destroy man's faith and relationship with God. He succeeded to steal the faith of Adam as well as his dominion position upon the earth by deceiving him into believing in his lies. He is a liar and a thief from the beginning and is the father of all lies.

You see, after Adam had eaten from the forbidden fruit, he became egocentric, insecure and afraid. His relationship with Eve his wife was immediately affected. As a result, the finger pointing mind-set was activated and the blame-game born.

Does this explain the degradation of the human society - the absence of God's word in Man's daily life? You know, God's Word is called the Word of life. (1 John 1:1) We know that the source of Man's life is the spirit (cf James 2:26), but the spirit is sustained only by God's Word without which it starves and dies. Therefore, man must not live by bread alone but by God's Word.

The devil is still at work even at this moment trying to steal the Word of God that is in your heart and to cause you to live by bread alone (i.e. according to your physical needs and desires, for bread is only to satisfy the physical needs of Man.)

But you are not just flesh and blood, you are a spirit, for God is a spirit (John 4:24) and you are created in the image and likeness of God.

You are called by God to live by faith and all Bible faith begins *with you trusting Christ as your Lord and Savoir. Jesus said, "It is the spirit that quickeneth; the flesh profiteth nothing: the words that I speak unto you, they are spirit, and they are life."* (John 6:63)

My prayer for you as you read on is that you may give the Word of God a central place in your daily life and to live by every word that proceeds from the mouth of God. Amen!

Chapter 4

WHO ARE YOU?

Most often, whenever someone is asked the question: *"who are you?"* People usually answer by saying their names. They may also add a phrase that says what they do in life and sometimes where they live or come from. Of course, the answers that are given in response to this question will vary depending on the occasion and context. But your name is not who you are, that is just what you are called. Your title or the job you do is also not a definition of who you are. Your title is simply a descriptive appellation of your rank or position in society.

Some people will think of who they are in terms of their race or nationality. This also does not define who you are. But I believe that knowing who you are is connected to knowing what your Creator says about you. God is the only one that has absolute knowledge of who you are. Until you know who you are, you will believe anything that is thrown at you. And you will not be able to position yourself in the grace of God that is available to you for the fulfillment of your destiny. In simple terms, *you will miss the purpose for your life,* if you do not know who you are.

Permit me to remind you of the fact that the architects and inventors of our time are usually the only people that are most knowledgeable with regards to the nature and purpose of the object of their creation or invention. What they say about their work is what everyone goes with. It is in the same fashion that we never question the manufacturers of any machinery or appliance when it comes to its design and purpose.

Oh how foolish is the believer when he goes to other sources but to the Word of God his Creator for his identity. God is your Creator and He alone is truthful in what He says you are.

God is the source of absolute truth concerning your life. What we sometimes call truth is limited to our knowledge and understanding and as well as our experiences. Truth is not what comes from you or me; it is what God says it is. God has given us absolute truth and that truth is in His Word. Therefore, Truth is what God says in His Word. He says it for you and I to know and that by knowing we might find freedom. For *"ye shall know the truth, and the truth shall make you free."* (John 8:32)

2 Corinthians 5:17 goes to say that: *"Therefore if any man be in Christ, he is a new creature: old things are passed away; behold, all things are become new."*

Every believer in Christ is created anew by the power of the Holy Spirit. To be in Christ is to be born of the Spirit of God through the Word. The Bible says, *"Being born again, not of corruptible seed, but of incorruptible, by the word of God, which liveth and abideth for ever."* (1 Peter 1:23 KJV)

Also in John chapter 1 and verses 12-13 it says, *"But as many as received him, to them gave he power to become the sons of God, even to them that believe on his name: Which were born, not of blood, nor of the will of the flesh, nor of the will of man, but of God."*

And James 1:18 says, *"Of his own will begat he us with the word of truth, that we should be a kind of first fruits of his creatures."*

Identity in Christ

A true Christian is someone that is born by the Spirit of God. He has become a different person from what he was before the renewing influences of divine grace. It is in fact as though he were formed all over again, and born afresh in his spirit.

On the new birth experience, Matthew Henry (1662-1714) made this observation: *"God is the origin of this good work. It is of God's own will; not by our skill or power; not from any good in us, or done by us, but purely from the goodwill and grace of God."*

The means by which the new creation reality is experienced is the Word of truth, which is the gospel of grace. The gospel is the power of God unto salvation for everyone that believes.

But most Christians have not looked into the Word of God to fine out what their identity in Christ is.

God's Word is a Spiritual Mirror

Let me share a story with you that I believe will make this point clear. There's a nephew of mine called Sinclair. When he was about the age of three, he had a group picture taken of him and other kids during Christmas. He was living with my aunt and her kids at the time.

After the picture was developed and I was looking at it, Sinclair came by to look also. When I pointed to different kids in the picture and asked him to identify them, he said what their names were. But when I pointed to his image in the picture and ask him who that was, he said, *"I don't know."* Sinclair was able to identify every other kid in this picture except himself.

That puzzled me and I got to thinking about what could be the reason that he could not recognize himself in this picture. It was only after a while that I figured out that Sinclair might not have seen himself in a mirror since he came into that home. He was not tall enough to view himself in the mirror that hung on the wall. So, I concluded that, because Sinclair had not seen himself in a mirror, he could not identity his image in that picture.

You see, many Christians are like this little boy. They have not looked into the mirror of the Word of God to see who they are. Therefore they do not identify who they are in the midst of what the Word says. Unfortunately some Christians are quick to identify the lives of other Christians through the mirror of the Word but remain blind to what the Word says concerning them and are thus carried away by every wind of doctrine.

Your Purpose in Life is tied to Your Identity

> I pray that the eyes of your heart may be enlightened in order that you may know the hope to which he has called you, the riches of his glorious inheritance in his holy people, and his incomparably great power for us who believe.
>
> (Ephesians 1:18-19 NIV)

God's original purpose for you and me in salvation was that we might manifest His image on the earth. Those who are not in Christ cannot manifest His image; they are dysfunctional apart from Christ. But for those who are in Christ, the new birth restored God's image in them. As they grow and become mature in Christ, He makes them to conform to the image of His Son. Jesus is the express image of His person. Christ in you is seeking to express the image of His person as He did while He was in His earthly body. He has a clear purpose for your life and He wants to show it to you.

I would like to share a vision with you at this point of how God showed me my life's purpose. One Thursday morning, in the month of April 2004 while I was meditating on the Word, my spiritual eyes where enlightened and I saw myself in a vision. This was an internal vision, for my eyes were closed.

I saw that I was dressed in a military uniform. The closest I could describe how I was dressed is like the way the British Army officers dress for state ceremonies. I had a scepter in my hand but there was no cap on my head. I saw myself on the balcony of what seemed like a castle. This castle was on a hill and below it in a distance I could see a multitude of people of all classes and races. I looked at myself and I could not understand why I was dressed like that. But I noticed that among the multitude of people I saw, some of them were familiar to me even though I did not recognize any faces.

As I became curious and tried hard to look for any familiar faces, I noticed that these people needed help and my heart was stirred with compassion for them. I immediately turned around and went through the door to enter the castle, but I found myself entering and going through a very large warehouse. I did not see anyone nor did I hear any sound at all in this warehouse. As I looked around, I saw many bags of provisions with different labels on them. I some-how knew that these bags where packed with food to feed the hungry and to nourish the malnourished.

I walked through this huge warehouse and went through the back door into the parking lot at the back. I saw the same bags of provisions that I had seen in the warehouse loaded in trucks. There was nobody around. I went to the first truck and opened the door to see if there was someone in it but there was none. These trucks where loaded and ready to go. I entered the last truck I saw and wanted to drive to the people, then the vision ended.

The above vision has totally transformed my life and shaped my identity in Christ. God was clearly showing me His plans for my life by opening my eyes to see what He has prepared for me to accomplish in this life. His purpose for my life was revealed to me in this vision. I am in full time pastoral ministry today, thanks to this revelation from the Lord. I knew that I was called to the ministry many years before this vision, but it was only when I yielded to His will that I found His purposes for my life.

I know who I am and what I am called to do in life, because God has shown me His purposes for my life. I believe He wants to do the same for you because He cares about you. The Scriptures reveals that: *"For from him and through him and for him are all things. To him be the glory forever! Amen"* (Romans 11:36).

If you haven't received Jesus in your heart, do that right now. Accept Jesus as your Savior and make Him the Lord of your life. The very moment you do so, your spirit is reborn and brought into fellowship with the Father, the Almighty God. You would become a Child of God. This will then put you in a position to receive from Him by faith all the promises that are in His Word.

Romans 10:9-10 says,

> That if thou shalt confess with thy mouth the Lord Jesus, and shalt believe in thine heart that God hath raised him from the dead, thou shalt be saved. For with the heart man believeth unto righteousness; and with the mouth confession is made unto salvation.
>
> (Romans 10:9-10 KJV)

You Can Receive Christ right now By Faith through Prayer:

Prayer is simply talking to God. God knows your heart and is not as concerned with your words as He is with the attitude of your heart.

The following is a suggested prayer:

"Lord Jesus, I need You. I believe that you are the Son of God, and that you were raised from the dead. Thank You for dying on the cross for my sins. I repent of sin and I open the door of my life to receive You as my Savior and my Lord. Thank You for forgiving my sins and giving me eternal life. Take control of the throne of my life. Make me the kind of person You want me to be."

Does this prayer express the desire of your heart? If it does, I encourage you to pray this prayer right now and Christ will come into your life, as He promised. Amen!

Who Does God Say I Am?

The following biblical truths about our identity in Jesus Christ are derived from a few selected passages in the New Testament. Declare them over yourself in full assurance of faith. Declare the *I Am* Scriptures and internalize them through prayer and meditation first, then, do the same with the *I Have* Scriptures. I encourage you to do this over a 21 day period and your life will never be the same. Amen.

Who Are You?

- I am a child of God. (John 1:12)
- I am a branch of the true vine, and a conduit of Christ's life. (John 15:1-5)
- I am a friend of Jesus. (John 15:15)
- I am chosen, holy, and blameless before God. (Ephesians 1:4)
- I am redeemed and forgiven by the grace of Christ. (Ephesians 1:7)
- I am not under condemnation; I have been set free from the law of sin and death. (Romans 8:1-2)
- I am a fellow heir with Christ. (Romans 8:17)
- I am joined to the Lord and am one spirit with Him. (1 Corinthians 6:17)
- I am a new creature in Christ. (2 Corinthians 5:17)
- I am no longer a slave but a child and an heir. (Galatians 4:7)
- I am seated in the heavenly places with Christ. (Ephesians 2:6)
- I am God's workmanship created to produce good works. (Ephesians 2:10)
- I am a member of Christ's body and a partaker of His promise. (Ephesians 3:6; Ephesians 5:30)
- I am a citizen of heaven. (Philippians 3:20)
- I have been justified and redeemed. (Romans 3:23-24; Romans 6:6)

- I have been accepted by Christ. (Romans 15:7)
- I have been called to be a saint (1 Corinthians 1:2; Ephesians 1:1; Philippians 1:1; Colossians 1:2)
- I have wisdom, righteousness, sanctification, and redemption. (1 Corinthians 1:30)
- I have become the righteousness of God in Christ. (2 Corinthians 5:21)
- I have been made one with all who are in Christ Jesus. (Galatians 3:28)
- I have been set free in Christ. (Galatians 5:1)
- I have been blessed with every spiritual blessing in the heavenly places. (Ephesians 1:3)
- I have been predestined by God to obtain an inheritance. (Ephesians 1:9-11)
- I have been sealed with the Holy Spirit of promise. (Ephesians 1:13)
- I have been made alive with Christ. (Ephesians 2:4-5)
- I have been brought near to God by the blood of Christ. (Ephesians 2:13)
- I have boldness and confident access to God through faith in Christ. (Ephesians 3:12)
- I have been made complete in Christ. (Colossians 2:9-10)
- I have been raised up with Christ. (Colossians 3:1)
- I have been chosen of God, and I am holy and beloved. (Colossians 3:12)

Chapter 5

THE ATONING WORK OF CHRIST

That Christ may dwell in your hearts by faith; that ye, being rooted and grounded in love, may be able to comprehend with all the saints what is the breadth, and length, and depth, and height; and to know the love of Christ, which passeth knowledge, that ye might be filled with all the fullness of God.

(Ephesians 3:17-19)

The atoning work of Christ through the cross is an expression of God's love for mankind. It is as we personally experience the breadth and length and depth and height of this love, that we become filled with all the fullness of God. This fullness of God is made possible through a living revelation of the completed atoning work of Christ on the cross; which is the covenant blessings of Calvary.

On the cross, Christ became sin for us so that we might become the righteousness of God in Christ. Jesus became one with sin (our sin) so that we might become one with righteousness, His righteousness. He identified with death and sin so that we might be identified with the Spirit of Life. He became a curse for us, so that we might inherit His blessings. He exchanged His life for ours so that we might receive His life to the fullest.

Christ's Incarnation

"And the Word was made flesh, and dwelt among us, (and we beheld his glory, the glory of the only begotten of the Father,) full of grace and truth" (John 1:14). Jesus had to live in the flesh so as to manifest the kind of life that we would experience after He had atoned for our sins and redeemed us by His blood.

The fall of Adam opened the door for Satan to sow corruptible seed into the heart of Man. While in the Garden of Eden, Adam submitted to the word of the devil, and the devil's seed of corruption was deposited into his spirit. His nature and character was then corrupted. So, with Adam as the father of the human race, this corruptible seed was then passed down unto the entire race. Thus all the descendants of Adam are born with a corruptible nature which is sinful.

But the atoning work of Christ makes a way for us to receive the blessings of the born again experience. Attesting to this fact, Watchman Nee (1903–1972) said, *"Our old history ends with the cross; our new history begins with the resurrection"* .in which case we are made partakers of the divine nature through faith in the power of the shed blood of Christ and the finished work of the cross.

The Bible says, *"His divine power has given to us all things that pertain to life and godliness, through the knowledge of Him who called us by glory and virtue, by which have been given to us exceedingly great and precious promises, that through these you may be partakers of the divine nature..."* (2 Peter 1:3-4)

Just as in Adam, all received Adam's nature of sin which brings death, even so in Christ are we made partakers of the divine nature, through the redemptive power of His precious blood. We have been engrafted into Christ by the operation of the Holy Spirit through *"the word of God, which liveth and abideth for ever*[10]*."*

All who are born again are new creatures created in Christ to be like God in righteousness and true holiness. The Bible says in Ephesians 4:24 *"... that ye put on the new man, which after God is created in righteousness and true holiness."* This new man is created after the likeness of the Heavenly Man. Thus, *"Our old history ends with the cross; our new history begins with the resurrection"* (Watchman Nee)

The Mystery of the Gospel

God's plan from the very beginning of time has always been to manifest Himself on the earth through Man. He created Adam and Eve in His image and likeness so as to relate with them as a Father. So, Adam was created a son of God (see

---

[10] 1 Peter 1:23

Luke 3:38). Adam's nature became poisoned with a corruptible thought (seed) from the devil and the knowledge of evil was activated resulting in the operation of the law of sin and death. Therefore, *"For this purpose the Son of God was manifested, that He might destroy the works of the devil."* (1 John 3:8)

The gospel is about our redemption, reconciliation, restoration of all things and the manifestation of the sons of God on the earth. The devil messed up with the first Adam and took the entire human race captive; then Jesus came as the Last Adam and paid the ransom for our freedom. The First Man disobeyed in the Garden of Eden, but the Second Man – Jesus, obeyed in the Garden of Gethsemane. The devil defeated the man from the dust, but the Heavenly Man won an eternal victory over the devil and his kingdom.

For Jesus to legally do all these wonderful works, He had to put aside His divinity and take on the form of a servant to His Father. He was Perfect Man and 100% Divine in His nature. But as the Last Adam with a mission to recover what the First Adam lost, Jesus had to face the Will of the Father in the Garden of Gethsemane. He did it as a man so that He may terminate with the Adamic sin (which is self-will). In Eden, Adam disobeyed God, so Jesus had to reverse that disobedience in Gethsemane through His obedience to God. He accomplished this by submitting His will to the will of the Father and by accepting to lay down His life through the death of the cross. He could only do this to redeem us as a Perfect Man. He could not use His divinity in the process. Of course, that was why His agony was very intense until His sweat was like great drops of blood (see Luke 22:44). Human ego was being dismantled and the seed of evil that was sown in Eden destroyed.

In my opinion, all servants of God must experience a personal Gethsemane in order to be worthy of that appellation. I believe this to be the key to the manifestation of the life of Christ in us and through us.

The Crucifixion

"But He was wounded for our transgression, He was bruised for our iniquities and by His stripes we are healed." (Isaiah 53:5) On the cross, the sin problem of man was settled by the blood of His crucifixion. By His shed blood on the cross Jesus atoned for our sins and reconciled us to God. He not only shed His blood for our sins but He died in our place so that we might be delivered from the nature and power of sin. Our old man was crucified with Him and the power of sin destroyed.

> Knowing this, that our old man is crucified with him, that the body of sin might be destroyed, and henceforth we should not serve sin. For he that is death is freed from sin. Now if we be dead with Christ, we believe that we shall also live with him.
> (Romans 6:6-8)

We are not only to have this knowledge but we likewise reckon ourselves to be dead indeed with Christ.

> For in that he died, he died unto sin once: but in that he liveth, he liveth unto God. Likewise reckon ye also yourselves to be dead indeed unto sin, but alive unto God through Jesus Christ our Lord.
> (Romans 6:10-11)

About the crucifixion, Watchman Nee made the following observation: *"The Blood deals with what we have done, whereas the Cross deals with what we are. The Blood disposes of our sins, while the Cross strikes at the root of our capacity for sin."*

> But if we walk in the light, as he is in the light, we have fellowship with one another, and the blood of Jesus, his Son, purifies us from every sin.
> (1 John 1:7)

On the cross, Jesus settled the issue of guilt and condemnation, and all unrighteousness through the washing by His blood. Hence, reconciling us to God and giving us a right standing with the Father in Christ. That is why the Bible goes to say, *"If we confess our sins, he is faithful and just and will forgive us our sins and purify us from all unrighteousness."* (1 John 1:9) Also, Hebrews 9:14 says, *"How much more shall the blood of Christ, who through the eternal Spirit offered himself without spot to God, purge your conscience from dead works to serve the living God?"*

His Burial

> Now that he ascended, what is it but that he also descended first into the lower parts of the earth? He that descended is the same also that ascended up far above all heavens, that he might fill all things.
> (Ephesians 4:9-10)

By Christ descending into the lower parts of the earth, He defeated Satan and destroyed his works over man and stripped him of all his powers. 1 John 3:8 teaches that, *"For this purpose the Son of God was manifested, that he might destroy the works of the devil."* And in Colossian 2:15 the Bible says, *"And having spoiled principalities and powers, he made a show of them openly, triumphing over them in it."*

Jesus ruined Satan and his works as it relates to us who are in Christ. Therefore, Satan has no power whatsoever over anyone that is in Christ. My dear brothers and sisters, Satan has no authority over your life. He was stripped of all his authority and all his claims of accusations against the sons of God. Jesus said in John 12:31: *"Now is the judgment of this world; now the ruler of this world will be cast out."* Amen. This is now a done deal and not something to take place in the future.

> Then I heard a loud voice saying in heaven, "Now salvation, and strength, and the kingdom of our God, and the power of His Christ have come, for the accuser of our brethren, who accused them before our God day and night, has been cast down. And they overcame him by the blood of the Lamb and by the word of their testimony, and they did not love their lives to the death.
> (Revelation 12:10-11)

The blood of Christ is the means by which all who are in Christ are redeemed, and it is in virtue of the efficacy of the atonement that we are enabled to be victorious over the powers of the devil. You and I are victors in Christ. Greater is He that is in us than he who is in the world.

The Resurrection

The resurrection of Christ from the dead was the demonstration of the victory over the power of the corruptible seed that was sown into the soul of man, and the dead works with which it held man in captivity. *"This is why it says: 'When he ascended on high, he led captives in his train and gave gifts to men.'"* (Ephesians 4:8)

Jesus destroyed the power of death and defiled its claims by His resurrection *(O death, where is thy sting? O grave, where is thy victory?*[11]*)*, thus translating us from the kingdom of darkness into the kingdom of His marvelous light. We therefore rejoice in Christ, *"Knowing that Christ being raised from the dead died no more: death hath no more dominion over him."* (Romans 6:9)

> For he has rescued us from the dominion of darkness and brought us into the kingdom of the Son he loves.
> (Colossians 1:13)

We who are in Christ are partakers in all that He went through on the cross and His victory over death and the kingdom of darkness is equally ours. His resurrection was for our sanctification, our deliverance and freedom from sin and all its bondages. When He rose from the dead, He activated and set in motion the law of the Spirit of life in Christ Jesus. That is why Paul the Apostle said: *"There is therefore now no condemnation to those who are in Christ Jesus, who do not walk according to the flesh, but according to the Spirit. For the law of the Spirit of life in Christ Jesus has made me free from the law of sin and death."* (Romans 8:1-2)

---

[11] 1 Corinthians 15:55

The Atoning Work of Christ

The Ascension

Jesus, after satisfying the condition for our redemption and making us acceptable to the Father and us adopted as sons of God, and joint heirs with Him; He ascended and sat at the right hand of God the Father in Majesty. *"Far above principality and power, and might, and dominion and every name that is named, and not only in this world but also in that which is to come: and has put all things under his feet, and gave him to be the head over all things to the church."* (Ephesians 1:21-22)

> … And hath raised us up together, and made us sit together in the heavenly places in Christ Jesus.
> (Ephesians 2:6)

We are seated with Christ at the right hand of God the Father. Our position in Christ is elevated; far above principalities and powers, and might and dominion and every name that is named and not only in this world but also in that which is to come. Hallelujah!

Seated with Christ, we have rest and we are reigning with Him in the heavenly places. This is the revelation of the kingdom of God amongst men; in that Christ completed His work of redemption by restoring the dominion position of man on the earth and a right standing with the Father, making us a royal priesthood to represent our God and also to reign in the earth.

> But you are a chosen people, a royal priesthood, a holy nation, a people belonging to God, that you may declare the praises of him who called you out of darkness into his wonderful light.
> (1 Peter 2:9)

The born again experience brings with it the restoration of all that Adam lost in the Garden of Eden. The born again believer is recreated in Christ and given the same position Adam had before the fall and even much more. So I can conclude that; the blessing which God proclaimed over Adam is now mine by virtue of the completed redemptive work of Christ. Yes, you too can personalize it for yourself, while internalizing it into your consciousness.

> Then God blessed them, and God said to them, Be fruitful and multiply; fill the earth and subdue it; have dominion…
> (Genesis 1:28)

Take Time to Praise God

Now then, take some time and worship the Lord for His immense love and sacrifice on the cross and for the redemption that was wrought on our behalf. He has redeemed us completely and restored us to the dominion position over the earth. We are not just saved from our sins, or the consequences and power of sin, but He has crowned us with glory and honor for heavenly citizenship and granted us access to the resources of heaven.

I thank You Lord for the blessings of Calvary.

Psalms 107:8-9 says,

> Oh that men would praise the LORD for his goodness, and for his wonderful works to the children of men! For he satisfieth the longing soul, and filleth the hungry soul with goodness.

And verses 15 and 16 say again;

> Oh that men would praise the LORD for his goodness, and for his wonderful works to the children of men! For he hath broken the gates of brass, and cut the bars of iron in sunder.

I thank You Lord Jesus for the cross where you died for my salvation. Oh! With all my heart, I thank You Lord for paying the full price to redeem me. You have brought me out of darkness into light, out of the shadow of death to the comforts of life, even that abundant life which is in Christ. I was bound but You have set me free and made me free. You broke the chains asunder and used them on my foe. Lord Jesus, You cut and opened wide the prison doors and You took captivity captive. I rejoice in Your victory, the victory of the cross.

Oh freedom is mine. For, "If the Son therefore shall make you free, ye shall be free indeed." (John 8:36) I am free indeed. Amen.

Chapter 6

KNOWING GOD

Psalms 103:7 says:

> He made known His ways to Moses, His acts to the children of Israel.

God Almighty is knowable and we can know Him in a very intimate way. It's not enough to know about Him, His acts or what He did in the past but we need to also know Him at a personal level. It's as we know Him and His ways that we can appreciate His deeds. You know, the ways of God are consistent with Himself. Knowing God's ways is likened to knowing His character. I believe that true knowledge of God and of His ways can only be received by divine revelation.

God does reveal Himself to us through the working of the Holy Spirit. The Holy Spirit sheds light in our spirit by divine revelation. Revelation is first of all received in the spirit of man and later is transmitted to the mind. Flesh and blood has very little to do with it. God may use a man as a vessel through which revelation may come, but it is the Holy Spirit that illuminates us in the knowledge of God.

For example, you may listen to an anointed message on tape which the Holy Spirit uses to illuminate spiritual truth; making it to become real to you in your spirit-man. Truth which was veiled before has now become yours by divine revelation and you can perceive it with your spiritual eyes. It's become so real and so clear that you know for sure its working reality.

This kind of revelation gives you the knowledge of God and of His ways, and such knowledge imparts the life of God into you in an indelible way that you may not be able to explain to another person. You just know that you know. The Holy Spirit has opened the eyes of your inner- man and you can see it and by faith you have taken hold of it.

The Character of God

In Exodus 34 and verses 6 to 8 the Bible says: *"And the LORD passed by before him, and proclaimed, The LORD, The LORD God, merciful and gracious, longsuffering, and abundant in goodness and truth, Keeping mercy for thousands, forgiving iniquity and transgression and sin, and that will by no means clear the guilty; visiting the iniquity of the fathers upon the children, and upon the children's children, unto the third and to the fourth generation."*

The above passage is very rich with revelations of the nature and character of God Almighty. Moses was invited by God to this meeting on the mountain. The Lord had asked him to present himself before Him with a new set of stone tablets like the first ones, so that He would write the Law on it.

The Law of the Old Covenant was written on tablets of stone, but in the New Covenant, God writes His laws on our hearts. God does this by the power of the Holy Spirit who is at work within us both to will and to do for His good pleasure. Just as Moses was invited to present the tablets of stone for God to write on; so are we invited by the Lord to seek Him with all our hearts. He calls us to come unto Him for a new heart. He is the One that gives us the new heart, but we have to present unto Him the heart that we now have; so that He may take away the heart of stone and we may receive a new one.

> A new heart also will I give you, and a new spirit will I put within you: and I will take away the stony heart out of your flesh, and I will give you an heart of flesh. And I will put my spirit within you, and cause you to walk in my statutes, and ye shall keep my judgments, and do them.
> (Ezekiel 36:26-27)

> This is the covenant that I will make with them after those days, saith the Lord, I will put my laws into their hearts, and in their minds will I write them.
> (Hebrews 10:16)

It was when Moses presented himself before God with the tablets of stone that God descended in the cloud to reveal His glory and made His attributes known to him. Exodus 34:5 say,

"And the LORD descended in the cloud, and stood with him there, and proclaimed the name of the LORD."

Matthew Henry commented on this verse, saying, *"God descended in a cloud, through a visible means of His presence, and manifestation of His glory. This manifestation speaks of His character; He draws near to consider those that humble themselves to walk with Him."*

> For thus saith the high and lofty One that inhabiteth eternity, whose name is Holy; I dwell in the high and holy place, with him also that is of a contrite and humble spirit, to revive the spirit of the humble, and to revive the heart of the contrite ones.
>
> (Isaiah 57:15)

O Lord, what is man, that he should be thus visited? Surely, man is very precious to God!

> And the LORD passed by before him, and proclaimed, The LORD, The LORD God, merciful and gracious, longsuffering, and abundant in goodness and truth.
>
> (Exodus 34:6)

The following exposition is a paraphrase from Matthew Henry's commentary.

"Here the Lord proclaimed the name by which He would make Himself known. He had made himself known to Moses in the glory of His self-existence, and self-sufficiency, when He proclaimed that name, I Am that I Am - The Revealing One."

"Now He makes Himself known in the glory of His grace and goodness, and all-sufficiency to mankind. The proclamation of His name shows the unlimited scope of God's goodness. God is good and

only God is good. He is not only good to those who love Him, but good to all. He is Jehovah, the Lord that has His being of Himself, and is the fountain of all being; Jehovah-El, the Lord, the powerful God, God of almighty power in Himself, and the origin of all power."

"God proclaimed His divine name Jehovah, Jehovah-El before the display of his goodness. He did it to teach us to think and to speak even of God's goodness with a holy awe, and to encourage us to depend upon His mercy. He is a merciful God. His greatness and goodness illustrate each other. That His greatness may not make us afraid, He shows us how good He is; and that we may not presume upon His goodness, we are shown how great He is."

The Self Revealing One

Many words are used in Exodus 34:6-8 to unveil and acquaint us with God's character. Again, with help from Matthew Henry's commentary, we will explore the rich content of these Scriptures.

First, God is merciful.

This speaks of His sympathy, and tender compassion, like that of a father to his children. This is first, because it is the first facet in all the illustrations of God's goodwill towards fallen man.

Secondly, God is gracious.

This speaks both of willingness, and kindness. It speaks of Him not only in terms of being compassionate towards His children, but having a sense of satisfaction in them, and also in doing good to them. Note that this is of His own goodwill, and not for the sake of any virtue in them.

Thirdly, God is long-suffering.

This is an aspect of God's goodness which our sin gives occasion for. He is longsuffering, that is, He is slow to anger, and delays the executions of His justice. He waits to be gracious, and lengthens out the offers of His mercy.

Fourthly, God is abundant in goodness and truth.

This speaks of plentiful goodness. It abounds above our need, above our conception. The springs of goodness are always full, the streams of goodness always flowing; there is goodness enough in God, enough for all, enough for each, enough for ever. It speaks of promised goodness, goodness and truth put together, goodness assured by promise. Hallelujah!

Fifthly, God keeps mercy for thousands.

This speaks first of mercy extended to thousands of persons. When He gives to some, still He keeps for others, and is never exhausted: And Mercy entailed upon thousands of generations, even to those that are far off to the outer most ends of the world; oh yes, the line of it is drawn parallel with that of eternity itself. His mercy endures forever.

Sixthly, God forgives iniquity, transgression and sin.

Pardoning mercy is shown herein, because it is in this that divine grace is most magnified, and because that is what opens the door to all other gifts of grace. He forgives offences of all sorts, iniquity, transgression and sin, multiplies His pardons, and with Him is plenteous redemption.

He is a just and holy God. For, He will by no means clear the guilty. He will not clear the impenitently guilty, those that go on still in their trespasses. He visits the iniquity of the fathers upon the children - especially for the purging of idolatry. Yet He will not keep His anger for ever, but visits to the third and fourth generation only, while He keeps mercy for thousands. This is God's name for ever, and this is His memorial unto all generations.

Worship, Our Response towards God

Every time God reveals Himself to anyone, the immediate response has been worship. Worshipers are those who have received a personal revelation of I Am that I am. We worship I Am, the God who is.

> And Moses made haste, and bowed his head toward the earth, and worshipped.
> (Exodus 34:8)

Won't you do like Moses? He made haste and bowed his head towards the earth and worshipped. Take some time to praise and worship Him for who He is.

> Jehovah, Jehovah God, merciful and gracious, longsuffering, and abundant in goodness and truth, Keeping mercy for thousands, forgiving iniquity and transgression and sin, and that will by no means clear the guilty.
> (Exodus 34:6-8)

Like Father, Like Son

Anyone seeking to know God ought to look at His Son. Jesus said, *"If you had known Me, you would have known My Father also."* (John 14:7)

> Left to ourselves, we arrive at a false knowledge of God, which begets fear and bondage and repels us rather than draws us to God. However, God has made a full and final revelation of himself, which makes Him understandable, accessible, and desirable. He has done so in His Son who made the worlds; humbled Himself to take on our flesh and blood, purged our sins, and now sits on the right hand of the Majesty on high. That Son is the Lord Jesus.
>
> -Roy and Revel Hession. Adapted from We Would See Jesus

Jesus is the expression of God's thought. He only spoke what He heard from the Father and did only what He saw the Father doing. He is the image of the invisible God and the brightness of the Father's glory. In John 14:7, Jesus said, "If you had known Me, you would have known My Father also; and from now on you know Him and have seen Him."

Pray now

My desire Father God is to know You and Jesus Christ whom You have sent. Help me to be diligent as I trust in Your faithfulness to grant me divine revelation of God's character. I know that Your will for me is that I may enjoy a closeer relation with You. Yes, I am hungry, Father God for that kind of relationship now. Thank You, Holy Spirit for being the One that reveals the Father to me. I welcome Your wonderful ministry in my life. Thank You Lord. Amen!

Chapter 7

THE GOODNESS OF GOD

No one is good but One, that is, God.
(Mark 10:18)

God is good and He alone is the source of all goodness. God is so good that His goodness surpasses our imagination. In Genesis Chapter 1, God demonstrated His goodness through creation. *"...and God saw that it was good,"* is repeatedly noted during the six days of creation.

God wants His beloved children to enjoy His goodness. So, He made us in His image and likeness and prepared good works for us to walk in (Eph 2:10).

God made us with a capacity to enjoy Him. He is good and enjoyable. He made all that is good so that we may enjoy.

Therefore, God richly gives us every thing for our enjoyment. (1 Timothy 6:17)

God gives in a way that does not hold back. But the devil manages to deceive us into believing that God is holding back from us. This was the lie Satan used to deceive Adam and Eve in the Garden of Eden and with it sin entered the world. It's an old trick of the enemy to say that God is holding back from you. Do not fall for that lie. Believe the word of God. Submit to God (align your life with God's word) and resist the devil and he will flee from you.

God did not spare His only begotten Son but gave Him up for us all, how will He not together with Him freely give us all things? (Romans 8:32) He gives the best, His very best.

Knowledge of His Goodness

Is there a personal need in your life? Draw near to Him right now in childlike confidence and make your request known to Him. Spend time in His presence to contemplate His greatness and goodness. Reach out in faith and receive everything that you may need. He wants to be good to you. For, God anointed Jesus of Nazareth with the Holy Ghost and power and He went about doing good. (Acts 10:38)

> His divine power has given us everything we need for life and godliness through our knowledge of him who called us by his own glory and goodness.
> (2 Peter 1:3 NIV)

As we walk with God, His goodness is revealed to us increasingly. As we plug-in unto the goodness of God, we would find out that His goodness is boundless. When we discover His goodness towards us, it draws us closer and closer to Him. His goodness and glory attracts us to Him. *"O taste and see that the LORD is good: blessed is the man that trusteth in him."* (Psalms 34:8)

In Matthew 19:17 Jesus said, *"No one is good but One, that is, God."* And in Matthew 7:11 He said, *"If you then, being evil, know how to give good gifts to your children, how much more will your Father who is in heaven give good things to those who ask Him!"*

The earthly ministry of our Lord Jesus Christ was a manifestation of the goodness of God to fallen humanity. Acts 10:38 says, *"how God anointed Jesus of Nazareth with the Holy Spirit and with power, who went about doing good and healing all who were oppressed by the devil, for God was with Him."*

Jesus would usually minister the goodness of God to people before they were convicted of their sin. Oh yes! The Scriptures teaches that it is the goodness of God that leads to repentance (Romans 2:4). One particular example we could take a look at is in Luke 5:1-8 where Jesus ministered God's goodness to Simon Peter.

> When Simon Peter saw it, he fell down at Jesus' knees, saying, "Depart from me, for I am a sinner, O Lord!"
> (Luke 5:8)

God Takes Pleasure in us

> The LORD taketh pleasure in them that fear him, in those that hope in his mercy.
> (Psalms 147:11)

God takes pleasure in His children. He loves to enjoy with us. We give Him pleasure by enjoying what He has given us. There is something we don't have to shy from and that is our rights to enjoy the blessings of our inheritance in Christ Jesus. We need to know who we are in Christ, and to have the most understanding about our inheritance in the Kingdom of God in order for us to enjoy its goodness.

Our knowledge of God is very important. For it is through our knowledge of Him who called us that we receive what God has made available for us in this life.

> His divine power has given us everything we need for life and godliness through our knowledge of him who called us by his own glory and goodness.
> (2 Peter 1:3 NIV)

Psalms 104: 10-15 says,

> "He makes springs pour water into the ravines; it flows between the mountains. They give water to all the beasts of the field; the wild donkeys quench their thirst. The birds of the air nest by the waters; they sing among the branches. He waters the mountains from his upper chambers; the earth is satisfied by the fruit of his work. He makes grass grow for the cattle, and plants for man to cultivate – bringing forth food from the earth: wine that gladdens the heart of man, oil to make his face shine, and bread that sustains his heart."

God wants us to be blessed. Blessings were the very first act that God did towards Man after He created them. It's God's nature to bless. He loves to bless His people. God wants you to be blessed so that you might be a blessing to others.

Ask God to bless you beyond your wildest dreams. Also learn to bless others beyond their wildest dreams for the glory of Him that redeemed us. Now then, consider the prayer of Jabez.

> And Jabez was more honourable than his brethren: and his mother called his name Jabez, saying, Because I bare him with sorrow. And Jabez called on the God of Israel, saying, Oh that thou wouldest bless me indeed, and enlarge my coast, and that thine hand might be with me, and that thou wouldest keep me from evil, that it may not grieve me! And God granted him that which he requested.
> (1 Chronicles 4:9,10 KJV)

Expectation from God

What kind of expectations do you have from God? Do you expect good from God? Do you expect God's blessings in your affairs? You do not need to listen to accusations of any sort. Set your mind on the word of God. Jesus Christ is the Word of God personified. Fill your thoughts with Scriptures that relate to your area of need or expectations. Build up your faith in the word of God. For faith comes by hearing and hearing by the word of God. Speak the word of God to yourself and see yourself become strong in faith.

God has given you the very thing you are expecting to receive. Cooperate with God and put to use the talents that He has given to you. Consider this parable.

> For the kingdom of heaven is as a man travelling into a far country, who called his own servants, and delivered unto

them his goods. And unto one he gave five talents, to another two, and to another one; to every man according to his several ability; and straightway took his journey. Then he that had received the five talents went and traded with the same, and made them other five talents. And likewise he that had received two, he also gained other two. But he that had received one went and digged in the earth, and hid his lord's money. After a long time the lord of those servants cometh, and reckoneth with them.
(Matthew 25:14-19 KJV)

God expects us to invest and be productive. He wants to give you spiritual capital for you to invest with. He is for investment. That's why He gave man all the seed bearing plants for food. *"Then God said, 'I give you every seed-bearing plant on the face of the whole earth and every tree that has fruit with seed in it. They will be yours for food.'"* (Genesis 1:29)

God gave man every seed bearing plant for food so that he would eat the fruit of it and plant the seed for a future harvest. He expects man to invest into his tomorrow by sowing. He wants you to succeed and He wants success out of you. But do you expect Him to prosper you? Do you expect Him to make His word good? You have to expect prosperity from God, before you can receive it. No farmer has ever sowed without the expectation of a harvest.

The difference between God's children who are experiencing His blessings and those who are not, is in their understanding of the principles of God's Kingdom (God's Economic System). In expectation of God's blessings in our life, we need to understand that He gives seed to the sower. Many Christians are not sowers but eaters. Become a sower and put to work the talents and gift that you have received. After you have done that, all you need to do is to align your heart and mouth with God's Word in expectation to receive. God is faithful to give you a harvest. You can not be a loser in God's system.

The Bible says, *"Then Isaac sowed in that land, and received in the same year an hundredfold: and the LORD blessed him."* (Genesis 26:12)

Know the Truth

God has given us absolute truth and that truth is in his Word. We have a responsibility to find out what the truth is and to build our life upon it. Jesus is the Word and the Word is the truth. The person of Jesus is what the Gospel is all about. He said in John 14:6, *"I am the way and the truth and the life. No one comes to the Father except through me."*

The scientist does his research because there is a truth and he believes that it can be found. Do like the scientist and be on the search for truth. Seek Jesus, because He is the way, the truth and the life.

In my experience as a believer in Christ, I have noticed that religion impresses man but God's goodness is experience through a living relationship and intimacy with God. God is not about religion (a set of dos and don'ts) but relationship. Intimacy with God does not produce religion but rather leads to reality. God is the essence of all reality. Therefore having a relationship with Him will lead you and me into all truth which is the core of all reality.

The truth is what God says in His Word. You can build your life on it and it will withstand the storms of life. Jesus said, *"Therefore whoever hears these sayings of Mine, and does them, I will liken him to a wise man who built his house on the rock: and the rain descended, the floods came, and the winds blew and beat on that house; and it did not fall, for it was founded on the rock. But everyone who hears these sayings of Mine, and does not do them, will be like a foolish man who built his house on the sand: and the rain descended, the floods came, and the winds blew and beat on that house; and it fell. And great was its fall."* (Matthew 7:24-27)

I strongly believe that, God's word is the boundary within which God's goodness is guaranteed. Amen.

Pray now

Lord, I confess that I am not a doubter; I am a believer. I believe in Your goodness, for there's none as good as You. You are good to all people and that includes me. For, there is no partiality with you. So I set my heart in expectation of the manifestation of Your goodness in my life. Surely, goodness and mercy shall follow me all the days of my life. Amen.

Chapter 8

GOD OUR FATHER

> Let not your heart be troubled; you believe in God, believe also in Me. In My Father's house are many mansions; if it were not so, I would have told you. I go to prepare a place for you. And if I go and prepare a place for you, I will come again and receive you to Myself; that where I am, there you may be also.
>
> (John 14:1-4)

Jesus came to introduce the Father to us. God is a Father, but we only become His children after we are born again. You see, children are either born into a family or they are adopted. But we have both experiences in Christ. We're born again children as well as adopted children of God. You may be asking yourself and wondering about the difference between becoming a child of God by adoption and by the new birth.

Well in Ephesians 1:4-5 the Bible says, *"According as he hath chosen us in him before the foundation of the world, that we should be holy and without blame before him in love: Having predestinated us unto the adoption of children by Jesus Christ to himself, according to the good pleasure of his will."*

You see, God made a decisive choice to adopt you as His child through Christ Jesus in accordance to His good pleasure. This was in relation to your history during which you were by nature a child of the devil, and you were heading towards perdition. He made this choice before you ever accepted Jesus as your Lord and Savior, but this adoption experience only became reality in your life the day that you received Christ and believed in the name of Jesus.

The moment you placed your faith for salvation based on the merits of Christ and received forgiveness for your sins, the Holy Spirit did an operation that recreated your spirit. You were born again and joint with Christ as one. (cf. 1 Corinthians 6:17)

Adoption then is in relation to our history before Christ in that God purposed to make us His children and the new birth is in relation to the divine act of our spirit-man being made anew, created in true righteousness and holiness after the image of God.[12] We were adopted and reborn at the same instant that we accepted and acknowledged Jesus as our personal Savior. Wow! What a mystery.

Therefore, as God's children, there is a place in the Father's house for each one of us. We have an inheritance prepared for

---

[12] Ephesians 4:24

us by Jesus in the Father's house. This is not just a promise for life in eternity as it is traditionally believed, but it is a place into the very presence of God.

We had lost our place in the Father's house. We were estranged from the Father because of sin; and the sin nature in man needed to be dealt with. So Jesus was manifested to deal with this problem. Therefore, He had to go to the Father's house after His resurrection to prepare a place for us, so that we can be at home with Him again as dear children of God. Jesus came as our Redeemer, to redeem us from sin and death, and also to restore us as children unto the Father. So that, *"where I am, you may be also"*. (John 14:4)

Father's Love

It was the Father's plan to send Jesus to us. Father God always loves us. His love is not just because of Jesus. He loves you and me for our own sake and that love is demonstrated regardless of any good in us. He sent Jesus because He loves us. He loved you and me independent of Jesus. That is why He demonstrated His love for us in that; while we were still in our sin, Christ died for us. (see Romans 5:8) Even before He created the heavens and the earth, He loved you. Your worth in the eyes of God is inexpressible. The Bible says, *"because of His great love with which He loved us, even when we were dead in trespasses, made us alive together with Christ (by grace you have been saved), and raised us up together, and made us sit together in the heavenly places in Christ Jesus"*. (Ephesians 2:4-6)

He created the earth and gave it to mankind as a love gift. He created us to enjoy the in the earth with Him.

> The heaven, even the heavens, are the LORD's; But the earth He has given to the children of men.
> (Psalms 115:16)

This knowledge is too wonderful for human comprehension. God's love for Man is so great that the psalmist had to say this: *"When I consider your heavens, the work of your fingers, the moon and the stars, which you have set in place, what is mankind that you are mindful of them, human beings that you care for them? You have made them a little lower than the angels and crowned them with glory and honor. You made them rulers over the works of your hands; you put everything under their feet."* (Psalm 8:4-6 NIV)

The Father's Heart

The parable of the prodigal son in Luke chapter 15 is one of those parables in Scriptures that God used to show me His Father Heart. In this parable, God is pictured as the compassionate Father that is always loving, always faithful, always forgiving, never controlling, never withholding anything good and always releasing and blessing. Father God is the ultimate giver of all good things.

> Every good gift and every perfect gift is from above, and comes down from the Father of lights, with whom there is no variation or shadow of turning.
> (James 1:17)

It was not hard for me to identify with the prodigal son as being rebellious and independent. That was easy as it was the central lesson of the parable; so I had believed. Of course, why not, for most preachers I had listen to on this subject focused their preaching on the prodigal son. But while reading Luke 1:1-3, it was like scales fell off my eyes as I read this:

> Then all the tax collectors and the sinners drew near to Him to hear Him. And the Pharisees and scribes complained, saying, "This Man receives sinners and eats with them." So He spoke this parable to them, saying:

I immediately saw that, Jesus was using this parable to address the accusations of the Pharisees and the Scribes. He was being accused of receiving sinners and eating with them. So in response, He used the older son in this parable as His answer to the accusations of the Pharisees and Scribes. But He did that to reveal the Father Heart of God and to expose the self-righteousness of the Pharisees and the Scribes. The Pharisees and the Scribes were likened as the angry, judgmental, resentful, jealous and afraid older son who did not know his father's heart nor did he have a proper understanding of his relationship with his father.

Though he was a son, he lived like a slave trying to earn his inheritance and his father's love.

About the older son, the Bible says: *"But he was angry and would not go in. Therefore his father came out and pleaded with him. So he answered and said to his father, 'Lo, these many years I have been serving you; I never transgressed your commandment at any time; and yet you never gave me a young goat, that I might make merry with my friends. But as soon as this son of yours came, who has devoured your livelihood with harlots, you killed the fatted calf for him.' And he said to him, 'Son, you are always with me, and all that I have is yours'"* (Luke 15:28-31)

Know your Birthright in Christ

Most Christians view God just like the older son in this parable. Many do not understand their God given rights in Christ and even those who have some knowledge to this regards, are confused with the doctrine of the sovereignty of God. They say things like *"God knows what I need,"* and *"God's time is the best or God cannot be manipulated."*

I was in this state of confusion in which I was trying to serve God as best as I could, and wishing for things to happen and passively hoping that God would intervene on my behalf and cause His will for my life to be fulfilled. I had little or no understanding concerning my inheritance as a child of God in Christ. I reasoned things out with my natural mind thinking that, if I try to be good and please God then He will automatically give me the desires of my heart.

On the other hand there are some of God's children who have some revelation on prayer - *"Ask, and it will be given to you; seek, and you will find; knock, and it will be opened to you"* (Matthew 7:7), and they are using it as a means to force the hand of an unwilling God to give them whatever they desire. God is willing to give you your inheritance. No one has ever worked to earn an inheritance. Once your name is in the will, the inheritance is yours. Jesus said these words: *"Do not fear, little flock, for it is your Father's good pleasure to give you the kingdom* (Luke 12:32). Do you know your birth right in Christ? Search the Scriptures and find out. Amen.

The Father's Restoration

Make no mistake my dear friend, sin has consequences. The first victim of any sin is the one committing the sin. *"The wages of sin is death."* Do not play with sin. Sin kills every time and it will kill you. The memory of sin will have a serious consequence on your life and the enemy can maximize on it to keep you in bondage for a very long time. There are more serious consequences to sin that only eternity would reveal its damage to humanity.

The prodigal son was restored but he had squandered his inheritance and there was none left for him. He had the rights of sonship but he had wasted his inheritance. For the older son, everything the Father has was his as well but he had never asked of the Father. He thought that he had to earn the love of the Father by being good and the Father would then reward him. He never enjoyed the full benefit of his sonship. May your case be different. And may you be wise in applying these lessons into your life. Amen!

What are your feelings about the Father? God is looking for opportunities to get you close to Himself, close to His glory and deeper into His grace in Christ. He is looking for ways to reveal His love to you from His Father heart. If you find yourself in the same situation like that of the prodigal son, please do likewise - repent. He came back to his senses and went home in repentance towards his father. Father God is a good Father. He is waiting for your return.

I have a feeling of goodness from God towards you. God is good and He loves you. He has always loved you. All that

He owns is yours in Christ. You are a joint-heir with Christ.[13] He is not holding back anything from you. The devil will not continue his lies in your life. Refuse to listen to those old lies. Resist the devil and he will flee from you.

God created Adam and Eve in His own image and likeness and the devil lied to them and stole their inheritance; he is still using the same tricks to steal and to keep you in the darkness of the religious systems. Say no to him and his lies. Tell him about your Father and His love for you and he will flee.

Be Encouraged

> For you know that we dealt with each of you as a father deals with his own children, encouraging, comforting and urging you to live lives worthy of God, who calls you into his kingdom and glory.
> (1 Thessalonians 2:11-12)

> May our Lord Jesus Christ himself and God our Father, who loved us and by his grace gave us eternal encouragement and good hope, encourage your hearts and strengthens you in every good deed and word.
> (2 Thessalonians 2:16-17)

The Father encourages us. He comes along side with us and helps us on. He cheers us up in what we are doing or going through at all times. He would give you encouraging words for others or for yourself.

---

[13] Romans 8:17

The Father comforts us when we are hurting or feeling alone; when we feel rejected or suffer lost of any kind. The Father does all these things through the Holy Spirit who resides in us. He who is the Comforter is also the Helper. He comforts and helps us in our down moments.

The Father urges. He shows us step by step how to live this life. Life is a challenge and the Lord has set an example that we should follow in His footsteps.[14] He loves you with an everlasting love. Only do no go away from His loving presence and life would be very sweet. Yes abundantly sweet.

Pray now

Father God, I acknowledge You as my Heavenly Father. I believe in Your unconditional love towards me. I acknowledge that Your plans for my life are the best. Let Your will be done. I repent of my waywardness and I am coming home to where I belong; to my Father's House. Amen

---

[14] 2 Peter 2:21

Chapter 9

THE GRACE OF GOD

And the Word was made flesh, and dwelt among us ...
full of grace and truth.
(John 1:14)

Jesus Christ is the same yesterday, today and forever. When He walked the face of the earth amongst men, He was full of grace; and that is still true today. Jesus is full of grace. His life on earth was the personification and expression of God's grace towards fallen humanity. Indeed, no one can encounter Jesus without experiencing God's grace.

When you receive Jesus as your Lord and Savoir, He comes into your life with all that He is. He is full of grace and truth; therefore you also received His grace when you received Him as Savior. *"And of his fullness have all we received, and grace for grace."* (John 1:16)

Saving Grace

> For by grace are ye saved through faith; and that not of yourselves: it is the gift of God: not of works lest anyone should boast.
> (Ephesians 2:8-9)

Salvation in Christ Jesus is by the grace of God and not of ourselves. The plan of salvation for fallen mankind was God's initiative and it's a gift from God. We are saved by His grace. Someone had defined grace as: *"God's Riches At Christ Expense."* Now, putting this in simple terms, it will mean that; *"grace is God's riches made available to me at the expense of Christ."* So I am entitled to God's riches in Christ because Christ has paid the bill. But understand that access into this grace is granted through faith.

Another definition for grace that is common among church people is: *"Grace is God's unmerited favor."* If that is the case, which I believe it is, *for there is no partiality with God* (Romans 2:11), then the grace of God must be the same for every person on the face of the earth. Yes, for the Bible teaches this exact same concept.

> For the grace of God that brings salvation has appeared to all men.
> (Titus 2:11)

If God's grace is available to everyone on the face of the earth, why are people not saved? Salvation is by His grace and this grace has appeared to all men, therefore all men are supposed to be saved. Isn't that right? But that is not the case, because man's response is needed for God's grace to work and to release the power of God into the life of men. This is where faith comes in.

My faith then is what determines how God's grace affects my life. Without faith, it is impossible to please God. Faith is what connects me to God's grace. Faith is the means of my response towards the finished work of Christ on the cross through his death and resurrection from the dead. The grace of God is independent of me. Christ paid the full price and made provision for my redemption over 2000 years ago. My response in faith appropriates for me what He accomplished by His death and resurrection. And this faith is a gift from God.

Grace alone would not save anyone. If that was true then everyone would be saved, since *"the grace of God has appeared to all men."* Therefore, salvation is *"by grace through faith."* Grace and faith must work together for salvation to be experienced by anyone.

This same principle will apply to healing, deliverance and prosperity. For the Bible says; *"who Himself bore our sins in His own body on the tree, that we, having died to sins, might live for righteousness — by whose stripes you were healed."* (1 Peter 2:24)

Visible Grace

Barnabas was sent out from the church in Jerusalem to help the new believers in Christ that were being converted as a result of the preaching of the saints that were scattered abroad after the persecution which arose with the death of Stephen.

The Bible says, *"When he came and had seen the grace of God, he was glad, and encouraged them all that with purpose of heart they should continue with the Lord."* (Acts 11:23)

The grace of God in the life of these disciples was such that Barnabas could see its operation. God's grace was perceived in this case and it caused gladness and encouragement to flow from the one that perceived it. If God's favor was with the people and it was visible, I believe that I can appropriate that same favor by faith.

God's grace in your life should be visible in such a way that no one can be mistaken about it. May you reach out in faith and release the flow of God's grace into your life. It is a gift from God. Your faith is the agent by which you activate its manifestation in your life. Therefore, access into the grace of God is by faith. (Romans 5:2)

Great Grace upon

> And with great power the apostles gave witness to the resurrection of the Lord Jesus. And great grace was upon them all.
>
> (Acts 4:33)

The grace of God that was upon the apostles at this point in time was quantified as great grace. *"Great grace was upon them all,"* and that was the source of the great power with which they gave witness to the resurrection of the Lord.

The grace of God does empower. In the grace of God is found divine enabling. The supernatural working of God's power flows through faith and in conjunction with our understanding of God's grace as the source of its provision. For example, divine healing is provided for by grace (for Jesus paid the price – *by His stripes we were healed*), but our faith activates the flow of the healing virtue into our bodies.

This truth will also apply in the area of prosperity for the Bible says in 2 Corinthians 8:9; *"For you know the grace of our Lord Jesus Christ, that though He was rich, yet for your sakes He became poor, that you through His poverty might become rich."*

I heard Andrew Wommack's teaching on the balance of grace and faith, in which he said: *"Our faith only appropriates what God has already provided for by His grace"* Amen! That is the simple truth. God's resources are made available to us in Christ Jesus, but our faith is the channel through which these virtues flow from the realms of the spirit into the physical.

Empowering Grace

There was a time in the ministry of Paul that he prayed and asked the Lord to relieve him of the situation which he termed *"a thorn in the flesh."* The Lord answered and said to him; *"My grace is sufficient for you, for My strength is made perfect in weakness."* (2 Corinthians 12:9)

My understanding of this passage in the past has been that, God was saying to Paul something similar to; *"I will not deliver you as you desire, but My grace is sufficient for you to cope with this situation."* Even though this would be acceptable with most people's experiences as related to denying self and the formation of Christian character; on the other hand I believe that, God was reminding Paul of His provision by grace that is available through faith, and that His grace was sufficient to deal with the situation at hand. And also that God's power is in His grace to make perfect the areas in Paul's life where his human weakness or limitation was lacking. For he said; *"Therefore most gladly I will rather boast in my infirmities, that the power of Christ may rest upon me. Therefore I take pleasure in infirmities, in reproaches, in needs, in persecutions, in distresses, for Christ's sake. For when I am weak, then I am strong."* (2 Corinthians 12:9-10)

Commendation Grace

One day, as I was reading through the book of Acts, I came across this passage in Acts 14:26 which says; *"From there they sailed to Antioch, where they had been commended to the grace of God for the work which they had completed."* In a flash moment, I saw something that changed my prayer life for the better.

In acts 13:2 the Bible says; *"As they ministered to the Lord and fasted, the Holy Spirit said, 'Now separate to Me Barnabas and Saul for the work to which I have called them.'"*

You see, this group of leaders at the church in Antioch heard the Holy Spirit's instruction regarding Barnabas and Saul. They were called to do a particular work which was known to both Barnabas and Saul and obviously by the other leaders as well. With the knowledge of God's call and the work for which He has called them, one would assume that success was guaranteed. But they needed *commendation grace*.

My eyes where opened to see that, *"...having fasted and prayed, and laid hands on them, they sent them away"* was the commendation process spoken of in Acts 14:26. By fasting and prayer with the laying on of hands, Barnabas and Saul were being commended unto the grace of God for the particular work they were being called to do.

I saw that there is the grace of God for the work I am called to do and I need to commend myself unto that grace on a regular basis. The leaders prayed over Barnabas and Saul but I also believe that these men commended themselves unto this same grace regularly.

As Pastor of a congregation, I lead my people in commending the entire church unto the grace of God that is available for us to prosper and do His will in our community. I teach my people about the importance of trusting in the grace of God and commending ourselves unto that grace. It's amazing to hear and see the working of God's grace in the life of the church.

I believe that Paul the Apostle understood the importance of *commendation grace*, for that was very evident in his ministry. In Acts 15:40 the Scriptures say, *"And Paul chose Silas, and departed, being recommended by the brethren unto the grace of God."* We also see in Acts 20:32 how he commends other ministers unto God's grace.

Paul wrote in Galatians 2:9 saying; *"and when James, Cephas, and John, who seemed to be pillars, perceived the grace that had been given to me, they gave me and Barnabas the right hand of fellowship."*

Before the grace could be perceived, I believe that commendation unto that grace must take place. Do you believe that God's grace is sufficient and that it is available for you in Christ? Many of Paul's letters to the churches begin and end with a salutation of grace. Take time to read it for yourself.

There is God's grace available for you to succeed at any work He has called you to do. There is God's grace for your marriage to succeed. There's God's grace for you to succeed as a husband or a wife. There's God's grace for you to succeed as a father or as a mother to your children. There's God's grace for your ministry to prosper and be established. There's God's grace for you to see the vision God gave you to come into fulfillment. There's God's grace for you to complete whatever your assignment on earth is. God's grace is enough and there is no lack with it. It's all by His grace anyway and not of ourselves lest anyone should boast.

Commend yourself unto that grace just like Barnabas and Saul did. For the Bible says; *"From there they sailed to Antioch, where they had been commended to the grace of God for the work which they had completed."*

Always remember that you need to *"grow in grace, and in the knowledge of our Lord and Saviour Jesus Christ. To him be glory both now and for ever. Amen."* (2 Peter 3:18)

A Word of Prayer

Father, I thank you for your grace upon my life. I confess that your grace is sufficient for me to be victorious in life. I commend my life unto the working of that grace for the completion of your divine purpose in my life. Amen!

Chapter 10

CALLED FOR BLESSINGS

Blessed be the God and Father of our Lord Jesus Christ, who has blessed us with every spiritual blessing in the heavenly places in Christ.

(Ephesians 1:3)

The above passage of Scripture tells us that God has already blessed us. God is a Father that blesses His children with every spiritual blessing in glory. God has blessed us in Christ Jesus and that all these blessings are in spiritual form located in the realms of glory. This is a fact that is established in heaven.

> The blessing of the LORD, it maketh rich, and he addeth no sorrow with it
>
> (Proverbs 10:22)

What is a Blessing?

In the Bible (for example, in the Old Testament), a blessing is depicted as the bestowing of God's enabling grace for prosperity upon a person. When a person is blessed, it is a sign of God's grace upon him and also of God's presence with him. To be blessed means that a person walks in the path of God's plans for his or her life. The Scriptures say, *"'For I know the plans I have for you,' declares the LORD, 'plans to prosper you and not to harm you, plans to give you hope and a future.'"* (Jeremiah 29:11)

The manifestation of God's blessings could be clearly seen in the life of Biblical characters like Abraham, Isaac, Jacob, Joseph, David etc.

Concerning Abraham, God said to him:

> I will make you a great nation; I will bless you and make your name great; and you shall be a blessing. I will bless those who bless you, and I will curse him who curses you; and in you all the families of the earth shall be blessed.
> (Genesis 12:2-3)

In order to bless Abraham, God had to proclaim words of blessings over his life. God's empowering grace was released into the life of Abraham through words that God spoke in order to cause the manifestation of the blessing. This principle is clearly seen through out the Scriptures.

About Adam and Eve, Genesis 1:28 says,

> Then God blessed them, and God said to them, "Be fruitful and multiply; fill the earth and subdue it; have do-

minion over the fish of the sea, over the birds of the air, and over every living thing that moves on the earth."

God blessed Adam and Eve when He bestowed on them the ability *(i.e. the power to get results or power for a positive outcome)* to be fruitful and multiply; fill the earth and subdue it; have dominion over the sea, over the air and on the earth. Again God did this by speaking forth the blessing through words of command.

In like manner as with Adam and Abraham, God has already commanded His blessing over your life. You have been blessed. Ephesians 1:3 says that God has *"blessed us with every spiritual blessing in Christ Jesus."* Praise God! This is for sure, just like we know that we have been forgiven. God has blessed us with every blessing in the heavenly realms through Christ's finished work of grace.

The same God who has forgiven our every sin has blessed you and me in a similar fashion. He provided forgiveness in Christ Jesus before we were born again so that we can receive and experience it when we repent and turn to Him. So in likewise is the blessing provided.

If you believe in Jesus and have received his forgiveness, then in the same simple faith believe in His blessings in Christ Jesus. Just as we cannot see when sins are forgiven but the change of character in a forgiven soul; we can not see the spiritual blessings in the heavenly places manifest in our lives until we place our faith in the One who says we are blessed with all spiritual blessings in the heavenly realms.

God is pleased when we acknowledge the fact that He has blessed us. For the Psalmist affirmed this truth in saying, *"Praise the Lord O my soul and forget not all His blessings."* (Psalm 103:2)

Since God's blessings are in the heavenly realms and they are spiritual in nature, I have a role to play in the manifestation of God's blessing in my life on earth. Now, I know that through Christ Jesus, I have been given access to these blessings in the heavenly realms.

The Scriptures in Ephesians 2:4-7 say,

> But God, who is rich in mercy, because of His great love with which He loved us, even when we were dead in trespasses, made us alive together with Christ (by grace you have been saved), and raised us up together, and made us sit together in the heavenly places in Christ Jesus, that in the ages to come He might show the exceeding riches of His grace in His kindness toward us in Christ Jesus."

In Christ Jesus, God raised me up from the dead and I'm seated with Christ in the heavenly realms. Therefore, because I am in Christ and I am seated with Christ in the heavenly places, I have access to the blessings of God towards me that are in the heavenly realms where I am seated with Christ.

Activating the Blessing

Because I live in a terrestrial body and I am a son of man (of flesh and blood), I have the authority to command what is in the heavenly realms to manifest on the earth realm. For the Bible says, *"The heaven, even the heavens, are the LORD's; But the earth He has given to the children of men."* (Psalm 115:16). I am able to do this by declarations in a similar manner in which God operated when He created the worlds. God spoke and it came to be. So my Acknowledgement of God's blessings over my life through confessions of faith will activate its manifestation. It is simply agreeing with God concerning His blessings over my life and speaking it forth by faith. *"And since we have the same spirit of faith, according to what is written, 'I believed and therefore I spoke,' we also believe and therefore speak,"*[15]

Faith in God's blessings over your life will activate its manifestation when your heart and your mouth line up with the Word. Do you believe it? Can you see yourself blessed? Then believe it with all your heart. For, it is with the heart that one believes first, after which confession is made for its manifestation. Be single minded about God's will concerning your life. You have to believe with all your heart before you can see the manifestation of the blessing. The blessing of the Lord is an empowerment that is voice activated. Your tongue is a powerful resource to this effect. So use it wisely.

Jacob had to employ this same principle in his life. For God had blessed him by saying these words to him:

> I am the LORD God of Abraham your father and the God of Isaac; the land on which you lie I will give to you and your descendants. Also your descendants shall be as the dust of the earth; you shall spread abroad to the west and the east, to the north and the south; and in you and in your seed all the families of the earth shall be blessed. Behold, I am with you and will keep you wherever you

---

[15] 2 Corinthians 4:13

> go, and will bring you back to this land; for I will not leave you until I have done what I have spoken to you.
> (Genesis 28:13-15)

You see, God's blessing was operational in the life of Jacob from the day he received God's Word because he believed God. The blessing was working in his life throughout while he worked for Laban. But he had to invoke the blessing when he was about to face his brother, Esau. He did so by acknowledging God's blessing upon his life and speaking forth God's word saying:

> For You said, "I will surely treat you well, and make your descendants as the sand of the sea, which cannot be numbered for multitude."
> (Genesis 32:12)

Jacob had to keep God's word within his heart to meditate on it day and night. And when the occasion presented itself, he activated the covenant blessing by speaking forth the promises that God had made to him. You too can do likewise. Keep the Word in the midst of your heart and meditate therein, then speak out God's promises over your life and over the circumstances in your life. Then, let your heart's expectation be directed towards the positive outcome.

The Heavenly Man

> The first man was of the earth, made of dust; the second Man is the Lord from heaven. As was the man of dust, so also are those who are made of dust; and as is the heavenly Man, so also are those who are heavenly. And as we

have borne the image of the man of dust, we shall also bear the image of the heavenly Man.
(1 Corinthians 15:47-49)

In Christ, I am of the heavenly Man's kind. As Jesus is so are we in this world (1 John 4:17). God's favor was activated by faith and released through words in the life and ministry of the Lord Jesus and as well as that of the early apostles. We bear the very image of the Heavenly Man. We have His faith and power on the insight through the Spirit.

I believe in the blessings of God upon my life. I have the guarantee of the promises of God – the Holy Spirit. The gift of the Holy Spirit is the guarantee of the certainty of His promises. For, *His divine power has given unto me all that I need for life and for godliness.* This divine power is on the inside of me. The Holy Spirit has deposited His power in my spirit and He does help me to experience the manifestation of this power as a blessing. Therefore, I have the responsibility of stewarding God's blessing in my life. It's my calling in life – taking care of the blessing!

Get your Mind Renewed

For to be carnally minded is death, but to be spiritually minded is life and peace.
(Romans 8:6)

What we consider to be reality is seated in the mind of our consciousness. If our mind can receive divine truth and be grounded in it, then that same truth when experienced (i.e. when allowed to influence us) will alter our reality. The mind is a servant and it was created by God to serve us in getting us connected both with the spiritual and physical realms.

In Romans 8:6 the Bible says; *"for to be carnally minded is death, but to be spiritually minded is life and peace."* You will agree with me that being *carnally minded and spiritually minded* are opposites of each other. Therefore my mind can only go in one direction at a given time; meaning my mind is able to function like a switch. If my mind is set on carnal desires, the results would be death; but if my mind is set on spiritual desires, the results would be life and peace. In order for me to switch from being *carnally minded* to *spiritually minded*, I need to repent. Repentance is simply a change of course in my mind from being *carnally minded* to *spiritually minded*. If the latter happens, then my feelings and actions would then follow and not the other way around.

Knowing that to be carnally minded is death, I now have the responsibility to repent and renew my mind to become spiritually minded so that there would be life and peace flowing through my life always.

The Lord Jesus said in John 6:63; *"It is the Spirit who gives life; the flesh profits nothing. The words that I speak to you are spirit, and they are life."* Therefore being *spiritually minded* is to be Word minded. The words that Jesus spoke are spirit and they are life. Conversely, to be *carnally minded* is to be mindful of things that contradict the Word of God in my life. That would produce death. But the word of God is spirit and to be mindful of the Word would produce life and peace.

The blessings of God are spiritual. Therefore in order for you and me to be connected to the source of these blessings, *"the eyes of our understanding need to be enlightened; that we may know what is the hope of His calling, what are the riches of the glory of His inheritance in the saints, and what is the exceeding greatness of His power toward us who believe, according to the working of His mighty power."*[16] Our minds need to be renewed and transformed into the reality of the riches of the blessings in the spirit realm. These riches of the glory of His inheritance are on the inside of us – in our spirit-man.

> For those who live according to the flesh set their minds on the things of the flesh, but those who live according to the Spirit, the things of the Spirit.
> (Romans 8:5)

It is Finished

> For "who has known the mind of the LORD that he may instruct Him?" But we have the mind of Christ.
> (1 Corinthians 2:16)

God has given us access into the mind of Christ and in Him all things consist. Christ who dwells in us is possessor of all things. All things are under His feet – therefore under ours – for we are in Him. All things are already ours, because they are all His. How can we beg God to give again what He has already given? Can you pray that God would send Jesus to the cross for you? You would say no way. But why not? Because that would be assuming that His atonement for our redemption was not settled. But it is done and there is nothing more for Him to do. Jesus did all the hard part of the equation.

---

[16] Ephesians 1:18-20

The kingdom of God – the storehouse, the right hand of the Father is all within us. *Christ in you the hope of glory.* (Colossians 1:27) Don't ever beg God for those things already freely given in Him. To beg is to assume that you are not entitled to and also that He is not willing to bless you. But He had already blessed you. Believe it and appropriate all you need by faith! Just receive. It works. Hallelujah!

I once heard Charles Capps, the prolific faith teacher say this on TV: *"Grace is God's willingness to get personally involved to use His resources on my behalf even when I don't deserve it."* That to me is a resume of the blessing of Calvary. I believe that the secret to receiving things from God is to understand what God has already given by grace; then you can take it by faith. This is the faith that pleases God. And in this kind of faith lies our call for blessings.

1 Corinthians 2:9-10 says, *"Eye has not seen, nor ear heard, nor have entered into the heart of man the things which God has prepared for those who love Him. But God has revealed them to us through His Spirit. For the Spirit searches all things, yes, the deep things of God."*

Do you believe it? Walk then in the blessing, *"knowing that you were called to this, that you may inherit a blessing."* (1 Peter 3:9) As a believer in Christ, you were called to inherit the blessing of Abraham. The Bible teaches in Galatians 3:29 that: *"if ye be Christ's then are ye Abraham's seed, and heirs according to the promise."*

Ignorance of this truth is however the problem of all Christians who believe that the reason they're not doing well in life is because they are under the influence of a curse. Don't get me wrong, curses do exist and people are affected by them. And the devil is the enforcer of all curses.

But if you are born again and filled with the Holy Spirit, no one can place a curse on you and succeed! Even if they tried, it would not work. The Bible says *"no weapon fashioned against you shall prosper"* (Isaiah 54:17). Numbers 23:23 says, *"For there is no sorcery against Jacob, nor any divination against Israel…"* These words in Numbers 23:23 were uttered by Balaam, a man that was hired by Balak King of Moab in order to place a curse on Israel. He could not do it even though he tried very hard.

So you see, you don't need any repetitive deliverance or prayers for a curse to be lifted from your life, for the truth is, no one can succeed to place a curse on you without your permission. Jesus is the curse destroyer, (1 John 3:8) and He has destroyed every curse since 2000 years ago. So believe it and be free.

Pastor Chris Oyakhilome - Founding President of Christ Embassy, once answered a question on this subject and said: "Look at it this way, if you were to be cursed as a child of God, who is to see to it that the curse produces result? Is it the devil? You're more powerful than the devil. *"Greater is He that is in you than he that is in the world"* (1 John 4:4). Is it God? God is your Heavenly Father. Why would He supervise a curse against you? His *"thoughts for you are for good and not of evil, to give you a hope and a future"* (Jeremiah 29:11)."

Pastor Chris further observed that: *"The only Christian, however, who can be under a curse, is the one who is not in alignment with the Word of God. Many Christians are ignorant of the truths of the Word of God; therefore they are out of sync with the*

Word. When you ignore the Word of God, you take yourself outside the protective cover of God's grace, and that in itself is a curse."

Disobedience to God's word was the kind of advice Balaam gave Balak against the children of Israel (See Numbers 25:1-2; Revelation 2:14). But as long as you stay in the Word, you will be like a tree planted by the rivers of water; fruitful and productive for eternity. Praise God!

Someone may ask a question saying, *"What about curses that were operational before one become a child of God?"* My answer is that you should believe God and receive your freedom in the same way just like you did to be born again. (See chapter 5 of this book which deals with our redemption). Then you must align your heart and your mouth in sync with the Word God. Also, you must break all ties with your past; seek first the Kingdom of God and the blessing will manifest in your life. Amen! So be it.

My Response in Prayer

Father, I believe that Jesus the Christ paid the full price for my redemption, so that I might inherit the blessings of Abraham. Now, in humility of heart, I come before Your throne in repentance of heart and seeking to embrace the truths of the gospel. I repent of the sin of unbelief in the finished work of Christ. I confess that I am who God's word says I am, I can do what the Bible says I can do and I have what the Bible says I can have. Hallelujah. I am blessed. Amen!

About the Author

Pastor James is a gifted and dynamic Bible teacher who is deeply burdened for the believers, especially those he pastors, to know the truth about God's word, so that they may live a victorious life in Christ. His passion is to see the lost saved, the sick healed, the distressed relieved, the broken restored, the oppressed delivered and the discouraged empowered to victory.

His vision is to see whole families come to Christ and serve him with all their heart. Above all, as a missionary, he is committed to the world wide vision of the CMFI (Christian Missionary Fellowship International), to make disciples of all nations. Consequently, he works hard to establish a solid multi-ethnic congregation with the same missionary vision.

Pastor James is married to his sweet-heart Julienne Abigail who is a dynamic woman of God and a faithful partner in the ministry which God has entrusted unto them. They are blessed parents of two beautiful girls; Elizabeth Grace and Madeleine Shekinah.

Author's contact email: *ekortah@gmail.com*

www.ingramcontent.com/pod-product-compliance
Lightning Source LLC
Chambersburg PA
CBHW031257290426
44109CB00012B/624